Her Story

WOMEN WHOSE NAMES REMAIN WRITTEN FOREVER

Débora Rodrigo
Ana Rodrigo

Copyright
© 2022 Débora Rodrigo
© 2022 Ana Rodrigo
All rights reserved. It is prohibited, except as otherwise provided by law, the total or partial reproduction of this work, by any means or procedure, without the prior, express and written authorization of the authors.
ISBN: 979-8366-19484-6

To the women
who have impacted our lives
and who we remember
by name.

Contents

Abigail	60
Abijah	72
Adah	10
Ahinoam	56
Aksah	42
Anna	88
Apphia	128
Asenath	26
Azubah	70
Bathsheba	62
Bithiah	78
Chloe	116
Claudia	138
Damaris	112
Deborah	46
Elisabeth	86
Elisheba	36
Eunice	136
Euodia	130
Eve	8
Hadassah	80
Hagar	16
Hannah	54
Huldah	76
Jael	48
Jedidah	74
Jehosheba	68
Jemimah, Keziah and Keren Happuch	82
Joanna	92
Jochebed	30

Julia	126
Leah	22
Lois	134
Lydia	110
Mahlah, Noah, Hoglah, Milkah and Tirzah	38
Martha	94
Mary	84
Mary of Bethany	96
Mary of Galilee	100
Mary of Jerusalem	106
Mary of Magdala	102
Mary of Rome	124
Miriam	32
Naomi	50
Persis	122
Phoebe	118
Priscilla	114
Rachel	20
Rahab	40
Rebekah	18
Rhoda	108
Rizpah	66
Ruth	52
Salome	98
Sarah	14
Sheerah	44
Shiphrah and Puah	28
Susanna	90
Syntyche	132
Tabitha	104
Tamar	24
Tamar of Judah	64
Tryphena and Tryphosa	120
Zeruiah	58
Zillah	12
Zipporah	34

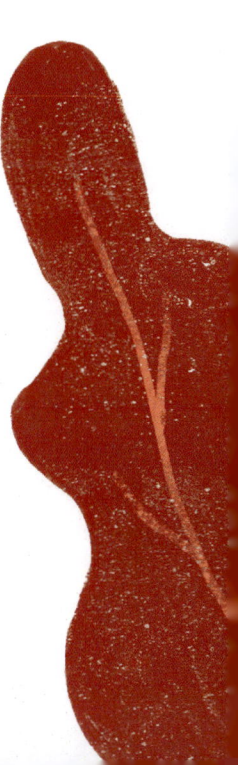

Foreword

"There is no longer Jew nor Greek, there is no longer slave nor free, there is no longer male and female; for all of you are one in Christ Jesus" (Apostle Paul to the Galatians).

When we Westerners of the 21st century approach Eastern stories written thousands of years ago that tell us about women, we travel to a galaxy far, far away. We move to worlds where women were not considered equal to men, not only in rights and opportunities, but also in their very essence, as they had come to be seen as inferior beings.

However, the Bible sets forth numerous stories that shake those conceptions more than we would imagine today. It does so not only as a breath of fresh air, but also as a liberating and dignifying breath signaling a long road ahead for humanity.

The God of Genesis described the women's oppression by men as a horrendous consequence of the evil generated by those who decide to worship their ego and desire for power (Genesis 3:16). The biblical story begins by showing that women's oppression is a curse that must be eradicated, although not all the characters in the Scriptures collaborated in this mission. But others do, and they are the ones who mark the inspired path for us.

To appreciate this divine breath more clearly, we must place the stories of the Bible in their hostile context. We must compare them with their environment and not with egalitarian treaties of the 21st century, which, as a matter of fact, owe much to the legacy of equality of the original Christianity of Jesus. Our culture does not grasp how transgressive Jesus became in his dealings with women. Jesus Christ is the standard that filters and measures everything we read in the Bible. Even his disciples were surprised that he talked to certain types of women.

He breaks taboos regarding customs and laws about women as impure or inferior people. He does it in grand gestures and with numerous details that often go unnoticed by the modern reader. All of this infuriated the religious hierarchy, just as it does today when a woman reflects God beyond each era's changing stereotypes and gender roles. But as Paul said, "if anyone is in Christ, he is a new creation. The old has passed away; behold, the new has come" (2 Corinthians 5:17).

If we read the stories chosen by the Rodrigo sisters in this book from the reality of their context, our astonishment over the dignity of women becomes adoration and gratitude. They brilliantly summarize very rich stories full of sobering layers in just a few lines. It is not an easy thing to do, and they do it very well, providing reflections that we must never forget about the character of God. The book's illustrations equally deserve an individualized pause for devotional reflection. Portraits just as impressive and varied as the different ways God approaches these women made in the Creator's image.

They are stories of mercy, restoration, and empathy that open paths not only for women but for all humanity. For each one of us.

Luis Marián

Eve

Life in the Garden of Eden was perfect. The sunbeams provided gentle warmth. The breeze was perfumed by the fragrance of flowers under a clear blue sky. The joyous sound of animals could be heard everywhere. Eve lived without worries, witnessing the course of nature, watching the trees grow and produce fruit, and enjoying the fresh streams of water.

A snake appeared between the branches of a tree: "Seriously? God doesn't allow you to eat the fruit of the trees?"

No, of course, this wasn't true; God had created a great variety of fruits so that people could enjoy different flavors and textures. And they were delicious. There was only one exception: among the many other trees, the one tree in the middle of the garden. That was the one that God had asked them not to eat from so that they wouldn't die.

"You won't die if you eat; you'll simply be like God," declared the snake, and then disappeared.

Eve thought about it. She had never felt like this before. The snake's words echoed within her. She was so confused. Actually, the fruit of the tree looked very good. What if eating it wasn't so bad? Then she did something she would regret for the rest of her life: she reached out, picked a piece of fruit, and bit into it. Since then, nothing has been the same again.

Eve knew firsthand what sin means. She suffered its consequences and knew pain. Tears accompanied her for the rest of her days. She came to understand that there was a reason for God's words. She wished so badly that she hadn't disobeyed. She felt ashamed. What a fool she had been! How she wanted to go back, erase what she had done. But it was no longer possible.

She was the first woman to experience God's forgiveness. The comfort of knowing that she was loved, despite her mistake and foolishness. God, whom she had profoundly failed, put aside His disappointment and embraced her. He gave her the gift of life inside her —her children— and the promise that one day, through a woman and the life within her, hope would come to the world, and the snake would be crushed forever. No more sin, no more pain. Never ever.

Genesis 2:18-25; 3:1-21

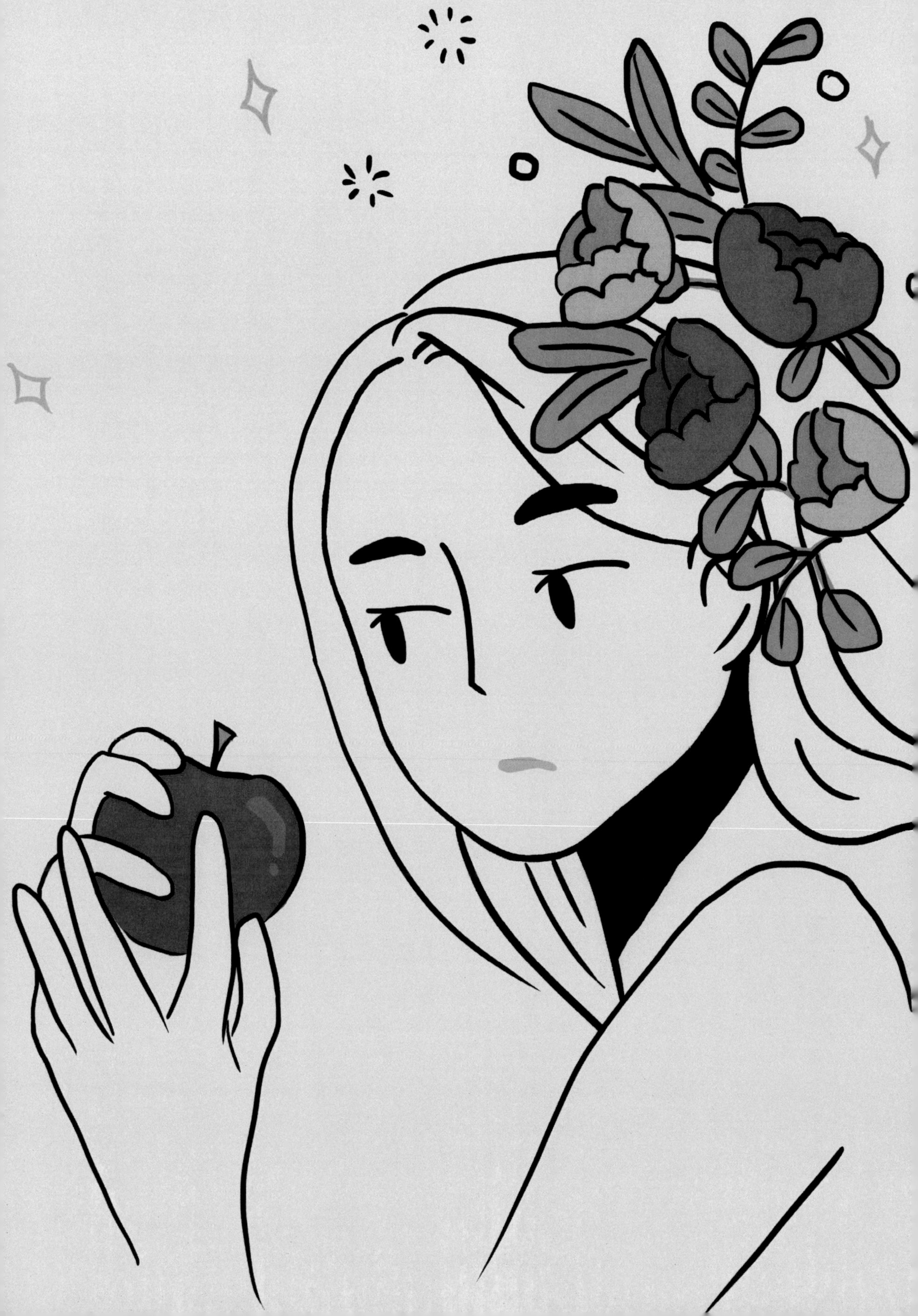

Adah

After God created the world and the humans in it, everything continued its rhythm. Life was spreading. Humans began to multiply and fill the earth, but so did pain and the consequences of sin.

Adah cried like she did every night, huddled in a corner, trying to swallow each sob, terribly afraid of waking up her husband. Lamech slept peacefully; it wasn't like he cared about the things Adah and Zillah seemed to give so much value to. He provided a home for them; he didn't see them as anything other than his own property, so he only expected them to behave as such. Yes, Lamech had married not one, but two women. That wasn't God's plan when He created man and woman, but that mattered very little to him, since he didn't care about other people's lives. Lamech prided himself on being a vindictive man and taking the lives of those who dared to mess with him. He had no qualms about raising his voice and threatening anyone nearby that he would kill them if they didn't do things his way. Adah was scared. She knew Zillah was too.

Many women since then have suffered the terrible prison of living in the shadow of a man who doesn't follow God's will. Some have died locked up without ever being able to see the light. Others have been able to get out. From the moment Eve bit into the fruit, God knew how much pain her wrong decision would bring. Perhaps for this reason He gave some women a very special gift: the gift of growing a baby in their womb and feeling life within. Adah lived on this adventure with her sons, Jabal and Jubal. In addition, she watched them grow into talented adults. Despite the pain of Adah's hard situation, God was always by her side and never stopped offering her the strength to endure. Suffering is often part of our lives, but we won't feel alone if we know that God is there, and life will be more bearable if we lean on the strength He offers us.

Genesis 4:19-24

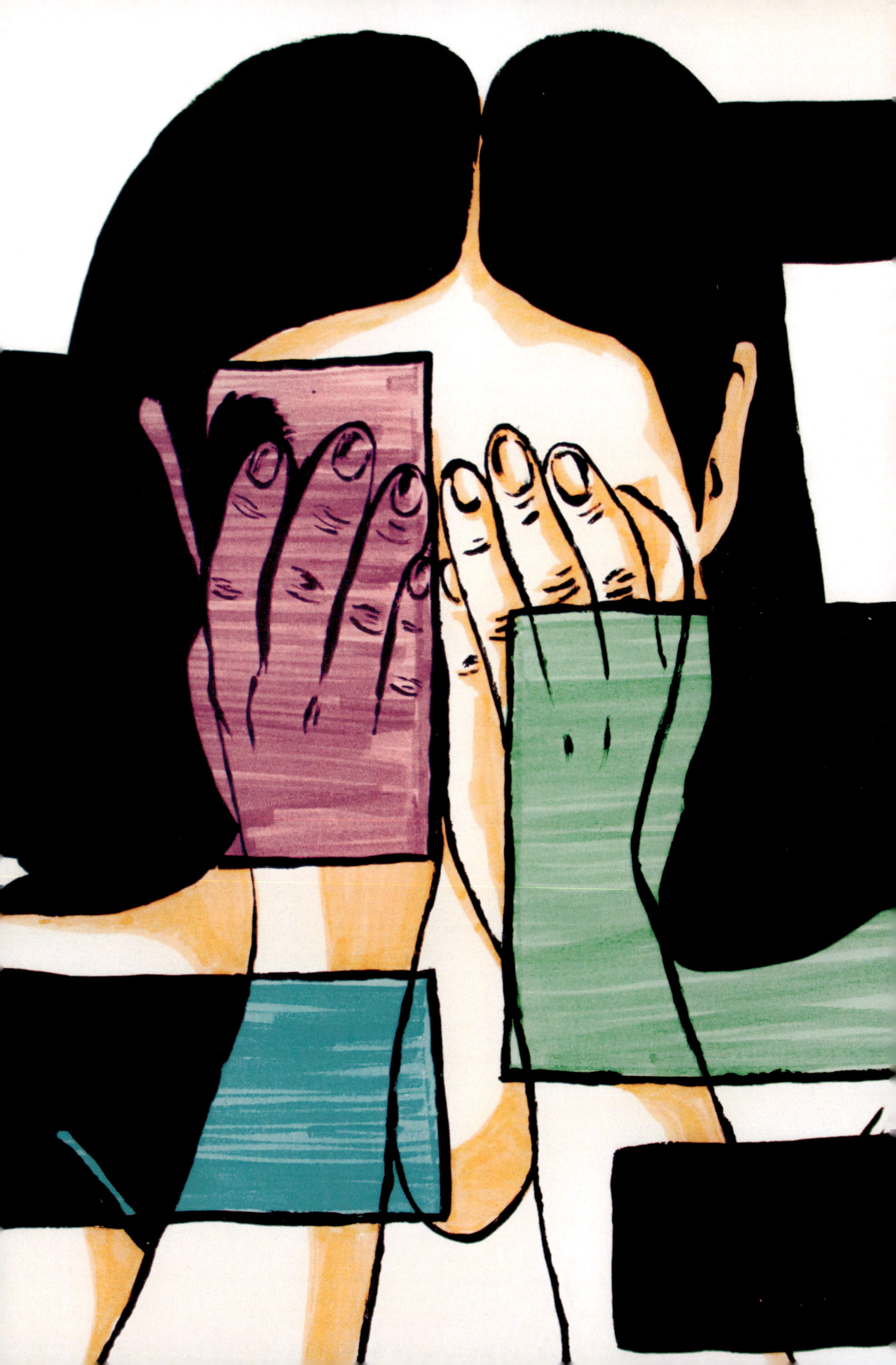

Zillah

Zillah listened in silence to her husband, Lamech. Even if she could, she wouldn't have dared open her mouth. There he was once again, standing with his head held high, his voice loud, and his laughter frightening. Everyone knew that Cain, Lamech's great-great-grandfather, had done terrible things. However, Lamech was proud to know he was one of his descendants. He believed that special bravery ran through his blood. Furthermore, he was fully convinced that God protected him, just as he had also protected Cain after what he did.

Zillah could barely meet Lamech's gaze as he spoke. She felt so small next to him.

"Hear my voice, Zillah," he repeated insistently, "and pay attention if you don't want the same thing that happened to the two who thought they could hurt me to happen to you."

Zillah knew exactly what he meant. Little did her life resemble the stories she had heard about Eden, about that close and warm God who only wanted to see His creation enjoying life. It was true that God had protected Cain's life precisely to prevent others from taking revenge by their own hand, but what about Lamech? Was God really protecting him in his pride? And if He was, did that mean that God would allow Lamech to place himself above Him and decide what he should do? He was full of arrogance, pride, and desire for revenge.

Zillah's life was not similar at all to the life she'd imagined for herself. She felt lost. She had many unanswered questions. She would've never thought that her husband would behave in such an atrocious way. Never before had she felt so insignificant and unimportant, as if she were nobody. Zillah tried to smile and respond lovingly to her two little ones. The hugs and laughter of her skilled Tubal-Cain and sweet little Naamah brought her back to reality for a moment. Zillah watched them grow up, and with all her strength, she wanted them to form united and loving families where God's goodness and love could rule.

Genesis 4:19-24

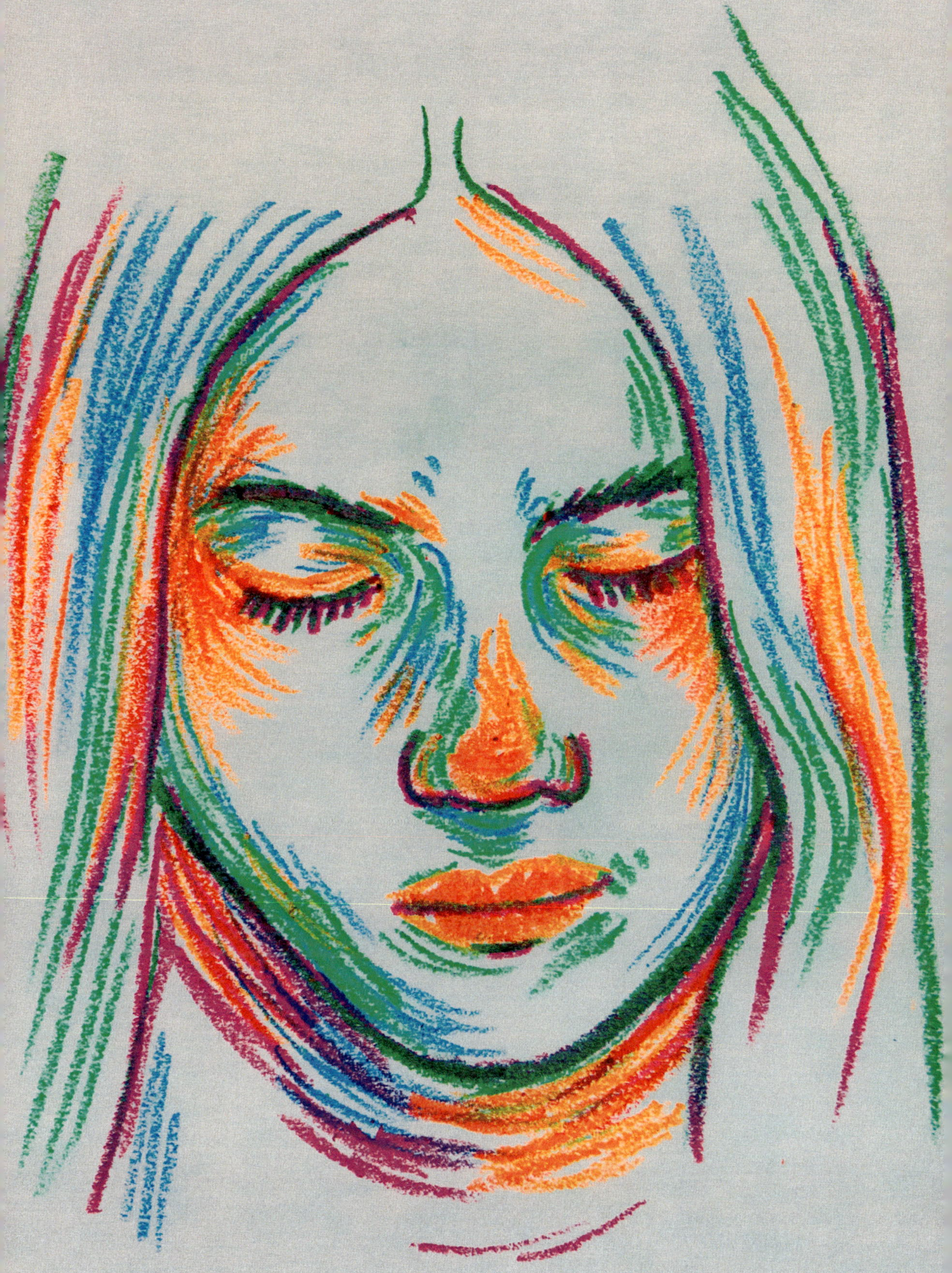

Sarah

Sarah lived with her husband, Abraham. They had been married for many years, and they lived lives that were pleasing to God. Sarah and Abraham had left everything to go to the place to which God had guided them. They'd been through many hardships but stood firm, honoring God with their lives. God knew they were a willing couple, so He chose them as the ones whose descendants would be God's people and bless many others. That was a great promise. Abraham and Sarah were very happy.

However, there was something that kept spinning in Sarah's head. She and her husband had no children. Sarah had always wanted children, but now she was very old, and it seemed impossible. Could it be that God would perform a miracle?

The years passed. Sarah was getting older and older. So then, Abraham and Sarah thought that God would use one of their servants' children to form that special offspring. Sarah was very disappointed. After such a long time dreaming of a child, this made her very, very sad. One day, Abraham entered the house and told her that God had promised him that He would not make a special people out of his servants but out of one of their own children.

"But we don't have any children!" Sarah replied. "Maybe you should look for another woman to have a child with so that God can make that special offspring."

Sarah was very wrong. Sometimes even people who love and follow God find it hard to fully trust Him. That was the case with her. But Abraham listened to her and looked for another woman. This plan only brought pain to his family. Sarah felt alone and distressed. She only wanted a family that would fill her heart and fulfill God's plan for them. But what she now had was a broken family that didn't please God.

Twenty-five years passed. Sarah was very old when she and Abraham finally had their son, Isaac. Sarah held her newborn son in her arms. She finally understood that God controls every detail. He doesn't need us to help Him when we don't see things clearly, and we just have to trust Him.

Genesis 12:8-20; 16:1-9; 17:15-21; 18:1-15; 21:1-13

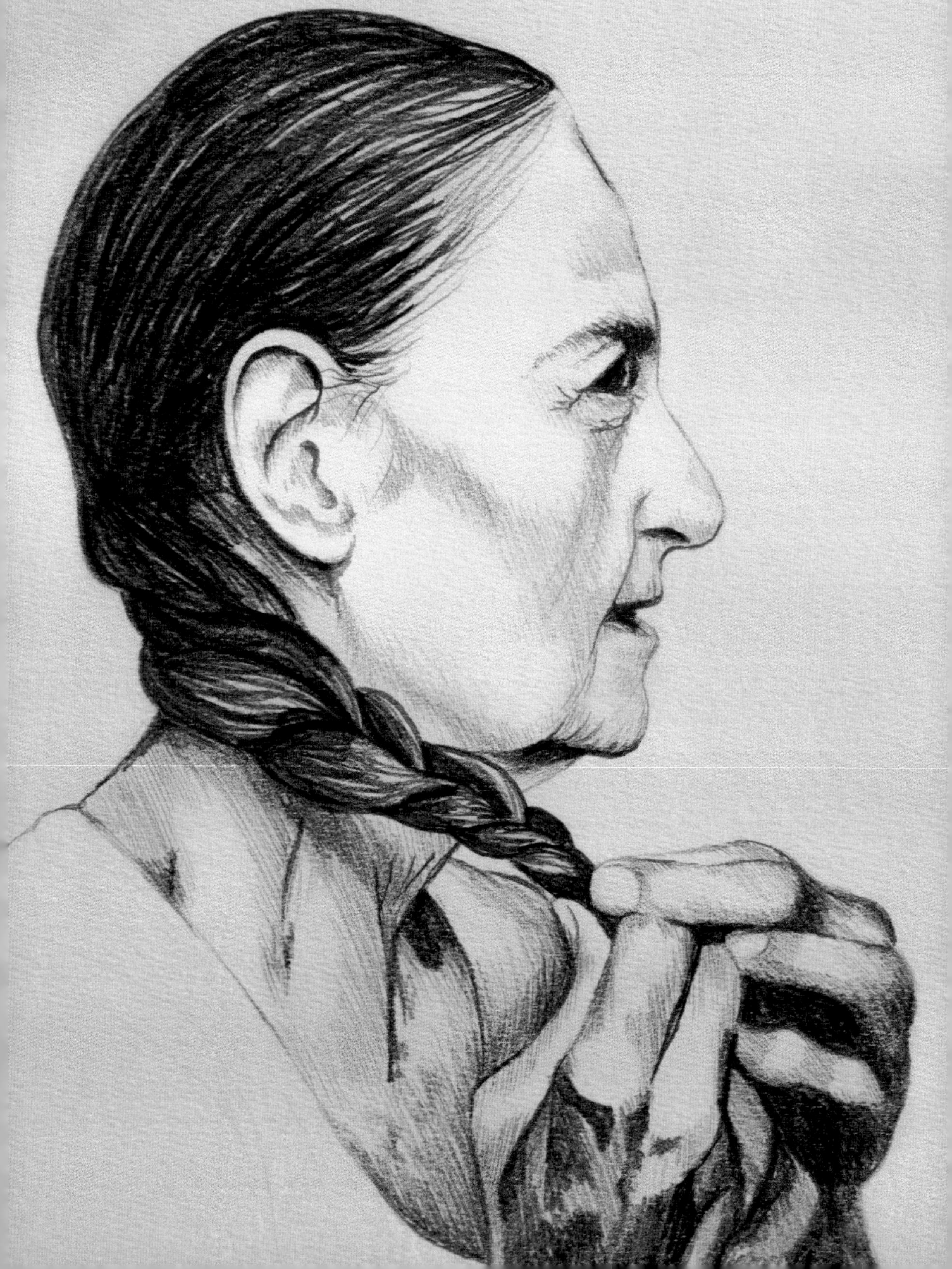

Hagar

Hagar was born in Egypt, but life took her to Canaan with the people God had chosen to form His own nation. Hagar would never forget her years with that family nor that terrible day, lost in the middle of the desert with her son Ishmael. She no longer had any of the bread and water that her husband had given her before throwing them out of the house. Many thoughts were going through her mind. She felt distraught, desperate, and completely alone. She didn't want to watch her son die. How had she reached this point?

Hagar's life had been difficult, like many other women sold into slavery. She had been the property of her owner, Sarah, for years. Things did not go as Sarah and her husband, Abraham, wanted, and they thought that if Hagar became — in addition to Sarah's slave — Abraham's second wife, everything would be solved. Back then, many men had more than one wife, which was not a good idea at all. But Hagar had no choice; after all, she was a simple slave. Her life didn't belong to her, and neither did her body.

The next few years were terrible for Hagar. She felt alone, lost, and powerless. Her owner, Sarah, had begun to mistreat her, and her husband showed no signs of love toward her. She felt that she was a problem and a heavy burden for everyone. She wanted to run away and escape from there.

It was for this very reason, finally, that they kicked her out of the house, to see if that would put an end to the uncomfortable situation. They sent her away with just a piece of bread and a skin of water. And she left as alone as she had always felt. But Hagar had learned something; she knew that God was watching her. Wherever she went, He never took His eyes off her. And God, who doesn't like injustice, didn't want to allow Hagar and Ishmael to die unjustly. So, God had Hagar find a water well and took care of them. What had been rejection and abandonment was now freedom and a future. Hagar would become a woman whose offspring would form a great nation.

Genesis 16:1-16; 21:9-21

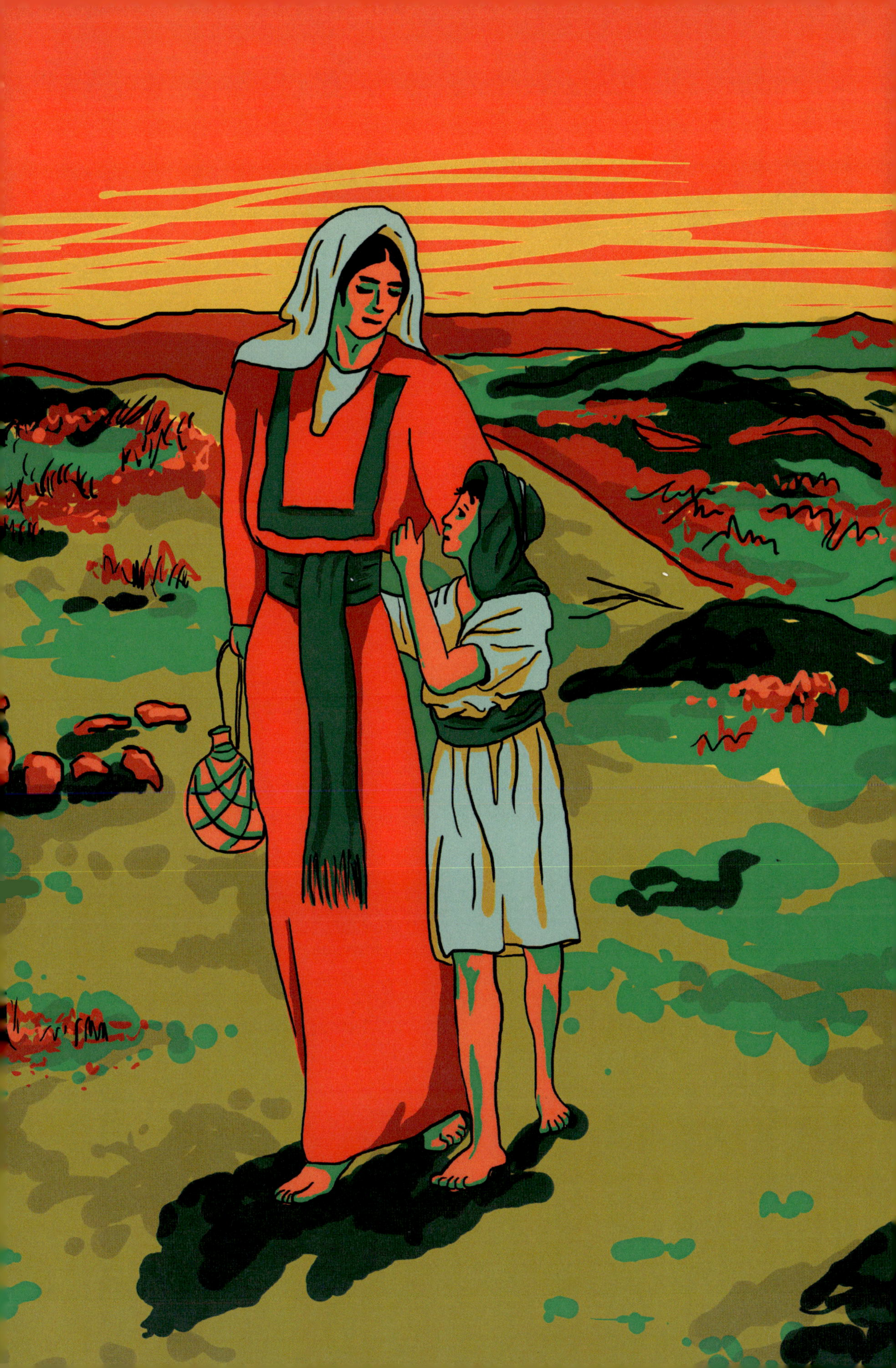

Rebekah

God was determined to gather and offer a close relationship to a special people. Isaac was ready to fulfill this mission, but he needed a wife with which to start a family, the family that God would bless as part of His own. No women in the area where Isaac lived loved God, so God led Isaac's servant to find Rebekah.

Rebekah was a beautiful and kind young woman who loved God. One day around the well where she used to go daily to collect water, Rebekah met a man who wasn't from the city. She offered him water to drink, not only for him but for his camels too. This man was Isaac's servant; when he met her, he realized that it was God who had brought him to Rebekah.

When Rebekah was asked if she would leave her family to marry an unknown man, she bravely said yes. It may seem strange to us today, but Rebekah understood it was God's plan for her life. She wanted God to do His will for her, despite the fear of leaving everything to start a new life in a different place and with a man she had never seen. She immediately got ready and went to meet her husband-to-be.

Rebekah married Isaac and lived with him for the rest of her days. There were happy times and difficult times, but God gave her the privilege of being part of establishing His special people. Rebekah and Isaac had two sons: Esau and Jacob. Jacob was Rebekah's favorite, and although she made some mistakes as a mother, God chose Jacob to continue forming that special nation. Of course, Rebekah's mistakes in raising her children had consequences; some of them put Rebekah through very difficult times, and she couldn't enjoy being with her beloved son as much as she would have liked. However, God is an expert at using His children's mistakes to create a special relationship with those He loves.

Genesis 24-29

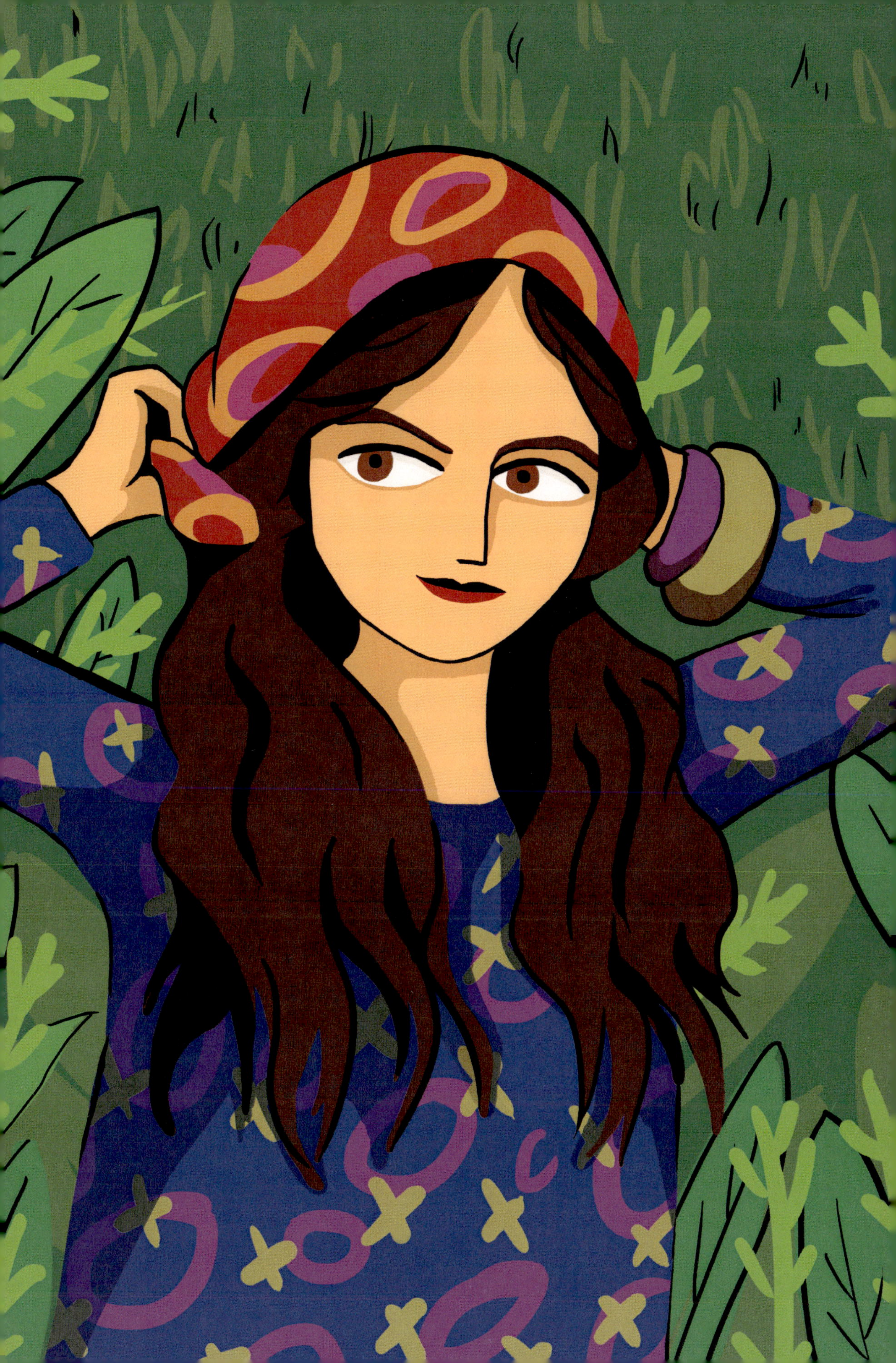

Rachel

Rachel was taking care of the family sheep the day she met Jacob. She felt butterflies in her stomach talking to him for the first time. From that day on, Rachel dreamed of becoming his wife and starting a family with him. Jacob shared that same dream and strove to make it happen. Rachel's father, Laban, didn't make it easy; he made Jacob work for seven years in exchange for receiving Rachel as his wife. No price would be too much for Jacob if the reward was to marry Rachel.

The wedding day finally arrived, the day that both Rachel and Jacob had waited for during those seven years. They were excited and full of joy. Finally, their long-awaited dream was going to come true. But neither of them could've imagined what Laban had planned for the wedding.

It wasn't Rachel who became Jacob's wife. Laban dressed Leah, Rachel's sister, as a bride and tricked Jacob into thinking it was Rachel. Rachel cried inconsolably as she thought of Jacob married to her very own sister. Her heart ached like you couldn't imagine. Of course, Jacob was very angry because of the deception. But there was nothing to be done. Jacob was married to Leah. Jacob also married Rachel, in exchange for another seven years of work for Laban. But, for Rachel, their marriage became a continuous competition with Leah, who was no longer her sister, but her main enemy.

Then, the second nightmare began. During the first years of their marriage, Rachel couldn't have children. Her sister Leah already had several, and Rachel deeply envied her for this.

God looked at Rachel's heart. An anguished heart, full of anger and despair. A heart that had been deceived and had learned to cheat and hold a grudge. A heart without joy. God loved Rachel and wanted to change her heart. Finally, Rachel got to have two children. One of her sons, Joseph, would save his entire family, including Leah's children, and bring restoration to a family broken by deception.

Genesis 29; 30; 31; 35:16-21, 24

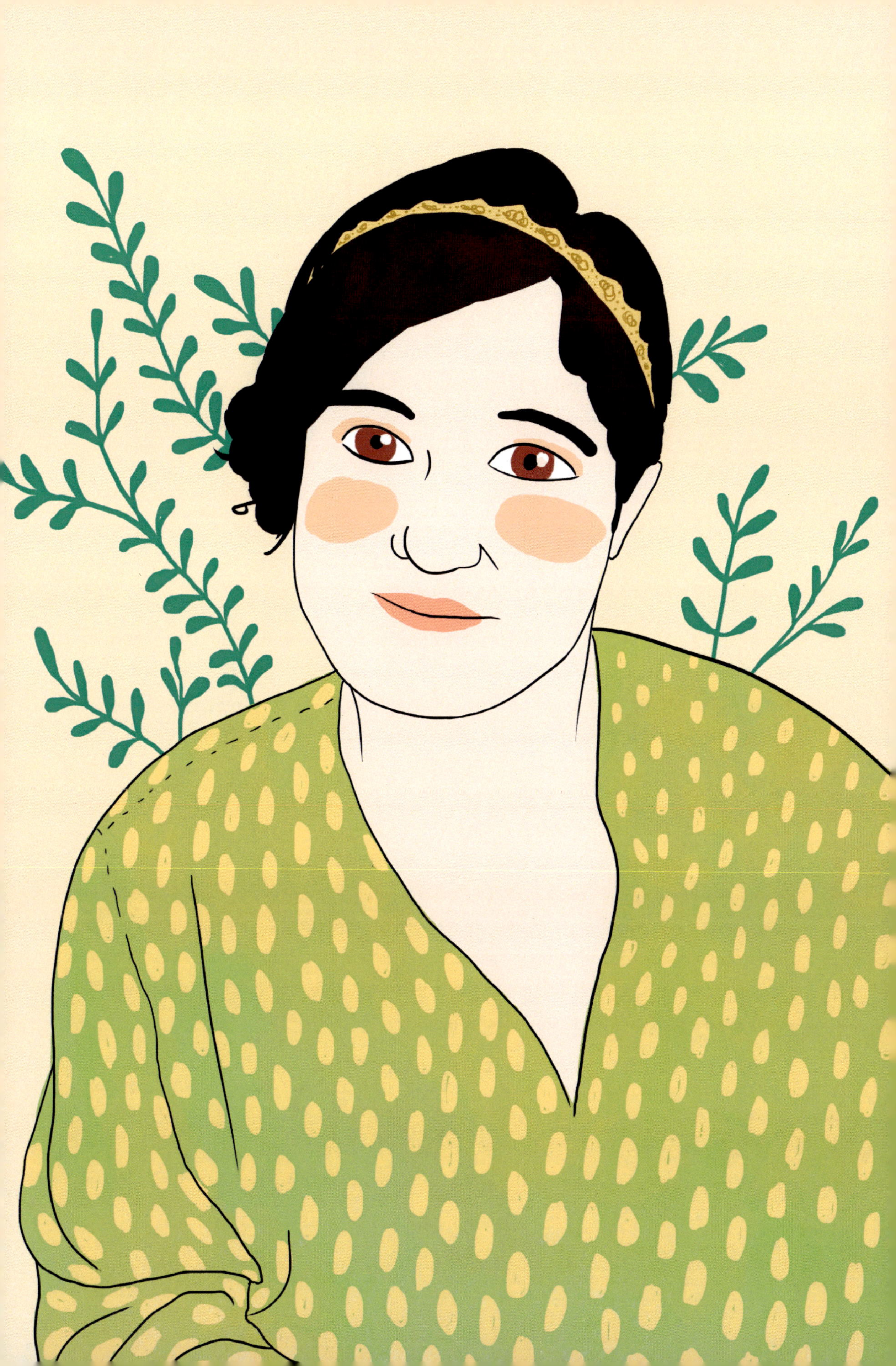

Leah

The day Rachel died giving birth to her second child, Leah became Jacob's only wife. Having a shared husband, although common in those days, made a woman's life much more difficult. Leah knew that her husband really loved her sister Rachel. But being Jacob's only wife didn't improve the situation. Jacob mourned Rachel's death for years and took it upon himself to make his suffering evident in her absence.

Leah was the older sister, but she had always lived in the shadow of Rachel, the prettier of the two. Leah thought she was lucky that her father married her to Jacob. She loved Jacob and strove from the beginning to be loved by him. But Jacob only had eyes for Rachel. Leah was devastated to be rejected by her husband, who frequently demonstrated who his favorite wife was, oblivious to the pain he caused Leah.

For years, she wanted to win Jacob's love through her children. With each pregnancy, she thought that her husband would finally love her because of that child. But that never happened. Leah prayed to God for her husband's love, but she learned to worship God despite not getting it. When Judah, one of her sons, was born, Leah said to herself:

"This time, I will praise God."

God watched Leah's broken heart and heard her prayers. It pained Him to see her suffering, and He felt compassion for her. He knew her husband would never love her as he loved Rachel and made her the mother of many children. She had eight children in all. One girl and seven boys. Seven sons who became great tribes of Israel. One of her sons, Judah, would be the one chosen by God to bring salvation to His people. Leah would be included in the genealogy of Jesus, whom God sent to comfort hearts and bring hope to so many who, like her, lived lives full of pain, deception, and injustice.

Genesis 29-31

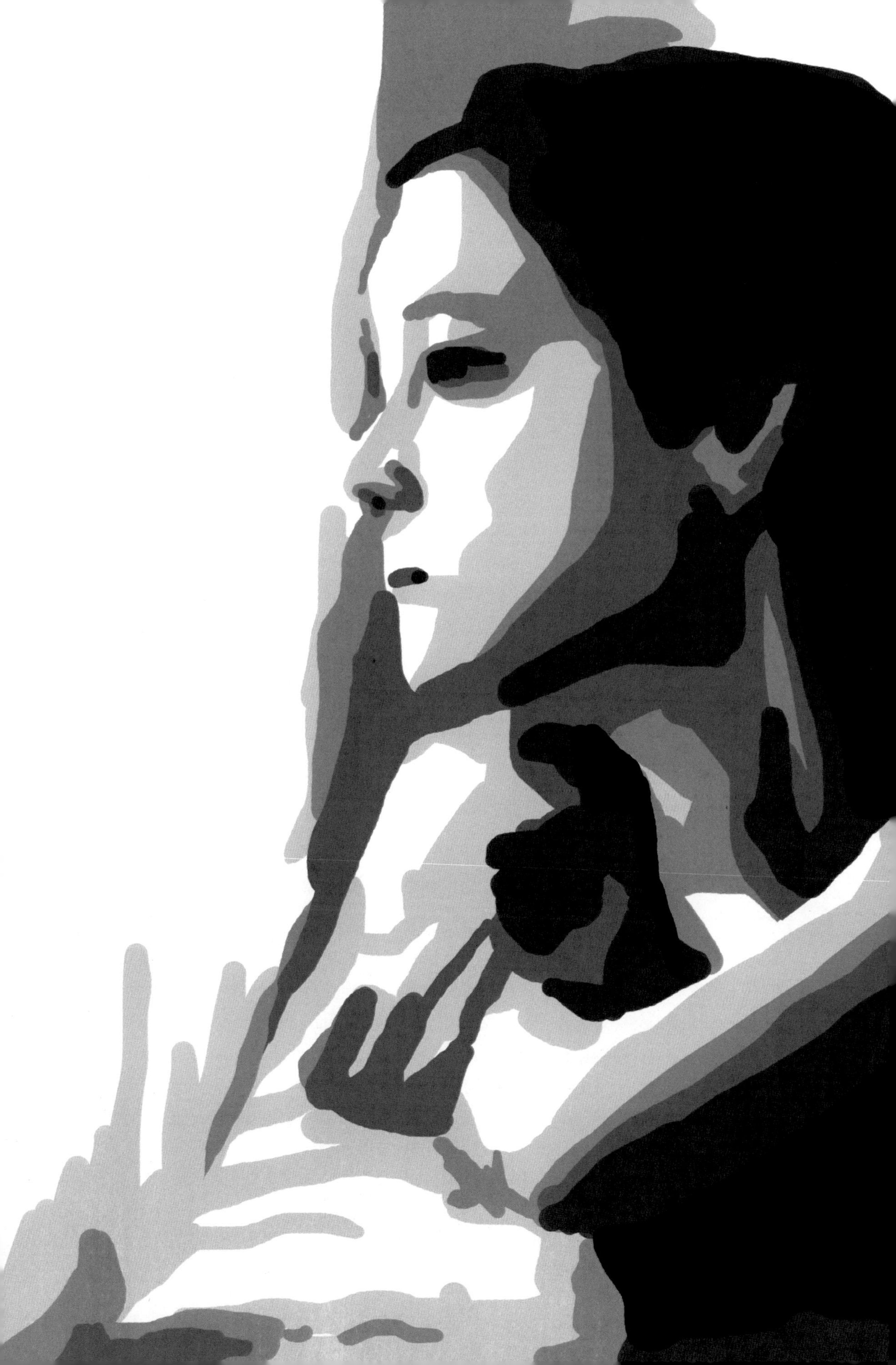

Tamar

Tamar didn't know God. She met Judah and his three sons, who were part of His chosen family. But to her, God was no different from the gods of other nations. Lifeless beings, represented by a figure of stone, wood, or metal, who were said to have power but were nothing more than a statue. God had nothing to do with those gods, but Tamar didn't know that.

It wasn't easy for her to know God when Judah married her to his older son, Er. Er wasn't a good husband; he wasn't really a good person at all. Tamar could hardly have known God through him. Due to his bad life and bad decisions, Er soon died. Tamar became a widow sooner than expected. Judah, following the laws of the time that forced relatives to take care of widowed women, married her to his next son, Onan. He was no better than his brother. He also wasn't a good husband, and Tamar wasn't able to meet the God of the children of Israel through him either. It wasn't long before Onan died as well. So, Tamar became a widow again.

This time, Judah didn't want to take responsibility for Tamar. He promised she could marry his third son, Shelah, in a few years. She was left alone and returned to her parents' house, waiting to remarry.

Although Judah tried to pretend that Tamar wasn't part of the family, to God, she was. She may not have known who God was, but God definitely did know who Tamar was, and He would take care of her, unlike Judah.

Years later, she realized that Judah had no intention of keeping his promise and devised a plan to trick him into accepting her back into his family. Tamar was making the wrong decisions. However, God didn't forget about her. He continued to count her as part of His special family and continued to work on her. Today, we remember Tamar as one of the few women mentioned in the Bible as part of the genealogy of Jesus, an unthinkable privilege not only for a woman but even more so for a foreign woman who wasn't born into the family of Israel.

Genesis 38

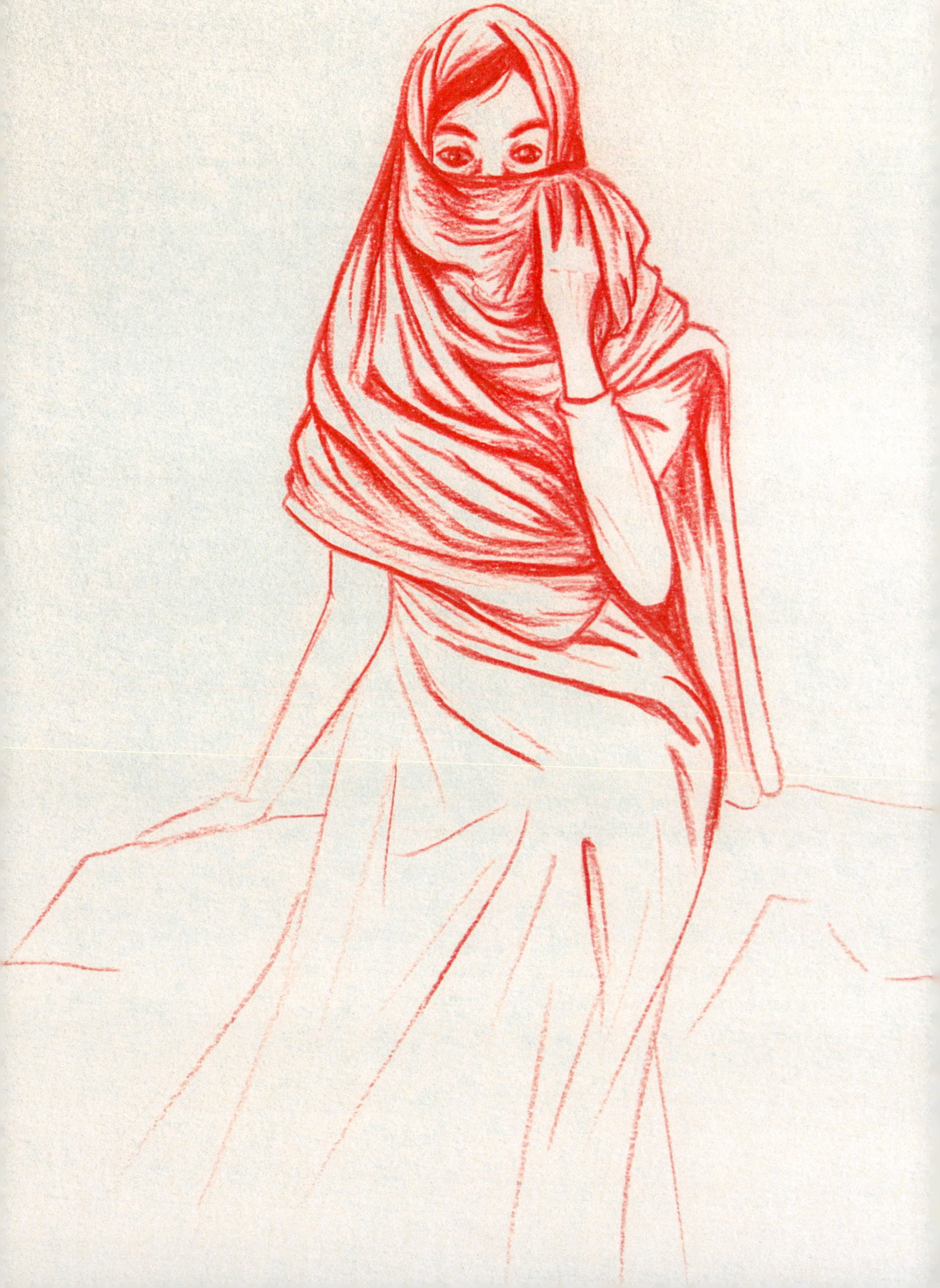

Asenath

The sun was shining brightly and warming Asenath's body that morning. Sitting in front of her house, Asenath thought about the sun and its importance for life. Without the sun, there would be no plants or food. Without the sun, clouds wouldn't form, and there would be no rain. Without the sun, the earth would be cold and uninhabitable. Without the sun, there would be no life. That is why the Egyptians, like Asenath, considered the sun a god to worship. Asenath had always felt privileged; her father himself was the priest of the Sun god. Ever since she was little, she had learned to worship and honor the Sun god as the one who allowed life and gave people everything they needed in this world to live. Always, until the day Asenath met Joseph.

Joseph wasn't an Egyptian; he was a Hebrew, and he belonged to the people of the Israelites. They believed in only one God. Joseph was handsome and intelligent, but, above all, he was an honest and good man. He had caught Pharaoh's attention and was made ruler over all of Egypt. It was then that Asenath married him. At first, Asenath didn't understand, but little by little, she realized that the God Joseph believed in was very different from the Sun god she had worshiped all her life. The Sun god was there, impassive, just as inaccessible every day. Totally unconnected to of their rituals and invocations. Joseph's God was a God who could be talked to, who would listen, and even respond! How was that possible?

Asenath saw daily how Joseph spoke with God and tried to live in a way that pleased God. Somehow, God made Joseph prosper. Joseph was joyful even though horrible things had happened in his past, and he was all alone in a foreign nation. Could it be true that this God was above the sun? Of course, Asenath had already realized that talking to the Sun god didn't make anything happen, and the sun rose and set in the same places every day. Joseph said that the sun was important, indeed, but he thanked God for its light and warmth. If it was God who made the sun shine and had control over life on earth, how wrong Asenath had been all her life! How wrong everyone around her was!

Genesis 41:45-51; 46:20

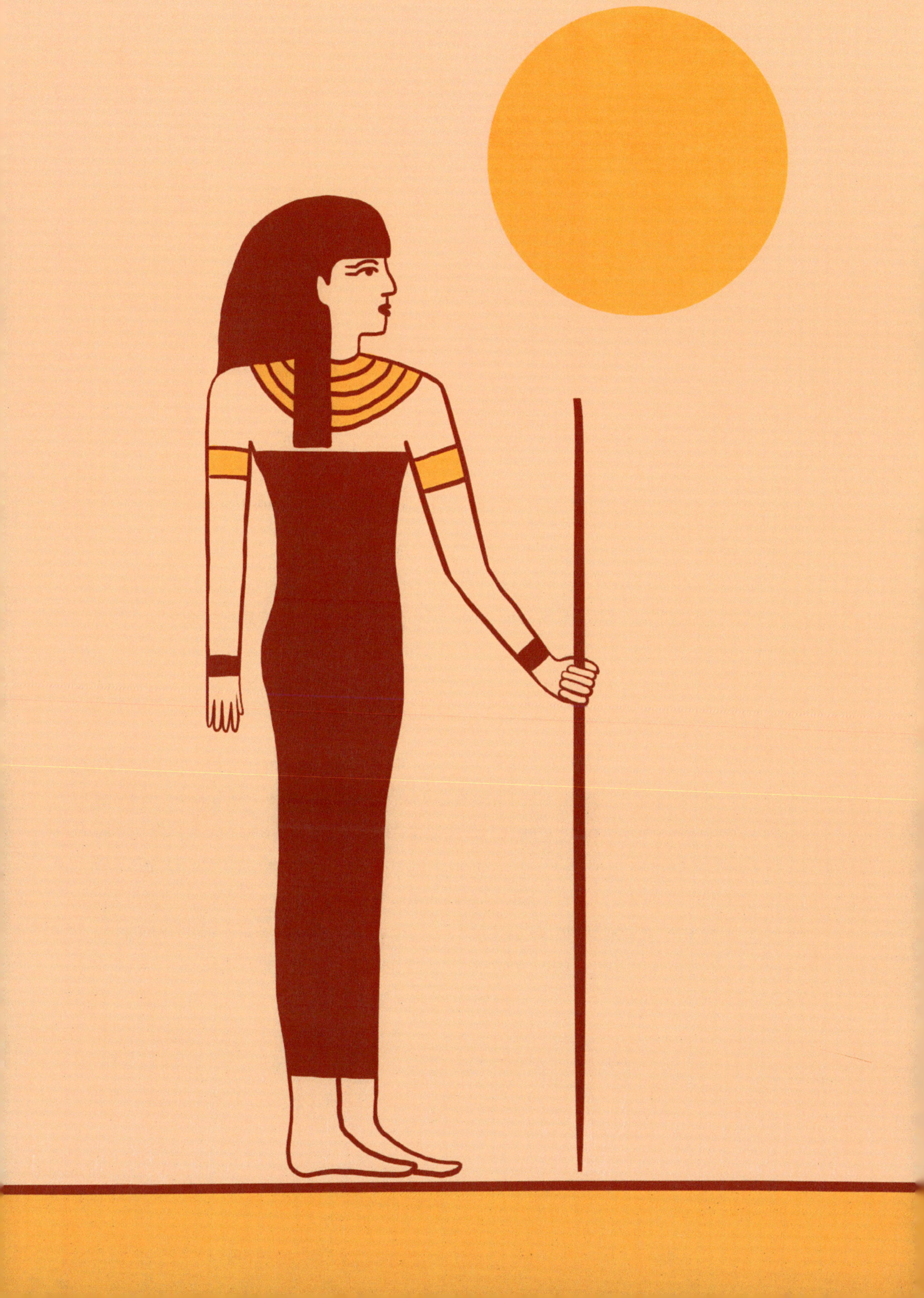

Shiphrah and Puah

Shiphrah and Puah were co-workers. They helped women with the birth of their children. Every day they were ready to welcome little babies in their arms and ensure they and their moms were healthy. One day, Shiphrah and Puah got an important order from Pharaoh.

Pharaoh was the ruler of Egypt, the place where they lived. Egypt was a prosperous and powerful nation that had become very important. Not everyone who lived there was Egyptian. The Israelites, God's people, also lived in Egypt, although the Egyptians had made them their slaves. Pharaoh was worried because he had realized that the Israelites were becoming more numerous, and he was afraid that one day they would decide that they didn't want to work for him for free anymore. That's why he thought he had to solve that problem.

When Pharaoh came to visit Shiphrah and Puah, his message was clear; from that moment on, they had to kill all the Israelite boys as soon as they were born, leaving only the girls alive. That way, the Israelites wouldn't be too numerous, and Pharaoh could continue to take advantage of them without fear. It was a terrible idea! Shiphrah and Puah also thought it was a bad idea, but they were in a very difficult situation. They had to obey Pharaoh. They couldn't refuse.

Shiphrah and Puah knew God and knew that He did not approve of Pharaoh's plans. They knew that God wouldn't like them to obey the orders they had received, but not complying could have very negative consequences for them. Although it was a very difficult decision, Shiphrah and Puah chose to do what God liked, even if it meant having to disobey Pharaoh and lying to him when he came to ask for explanations. They understood that God is above any order we receive, and their respect for God gave them the strength and courage they needed to do the right thing. Their decision could have brought them many problems, but God took it upon Himself to protect them from Pharaoh and rewarded them for what they had done.

Exodus 1:15-21

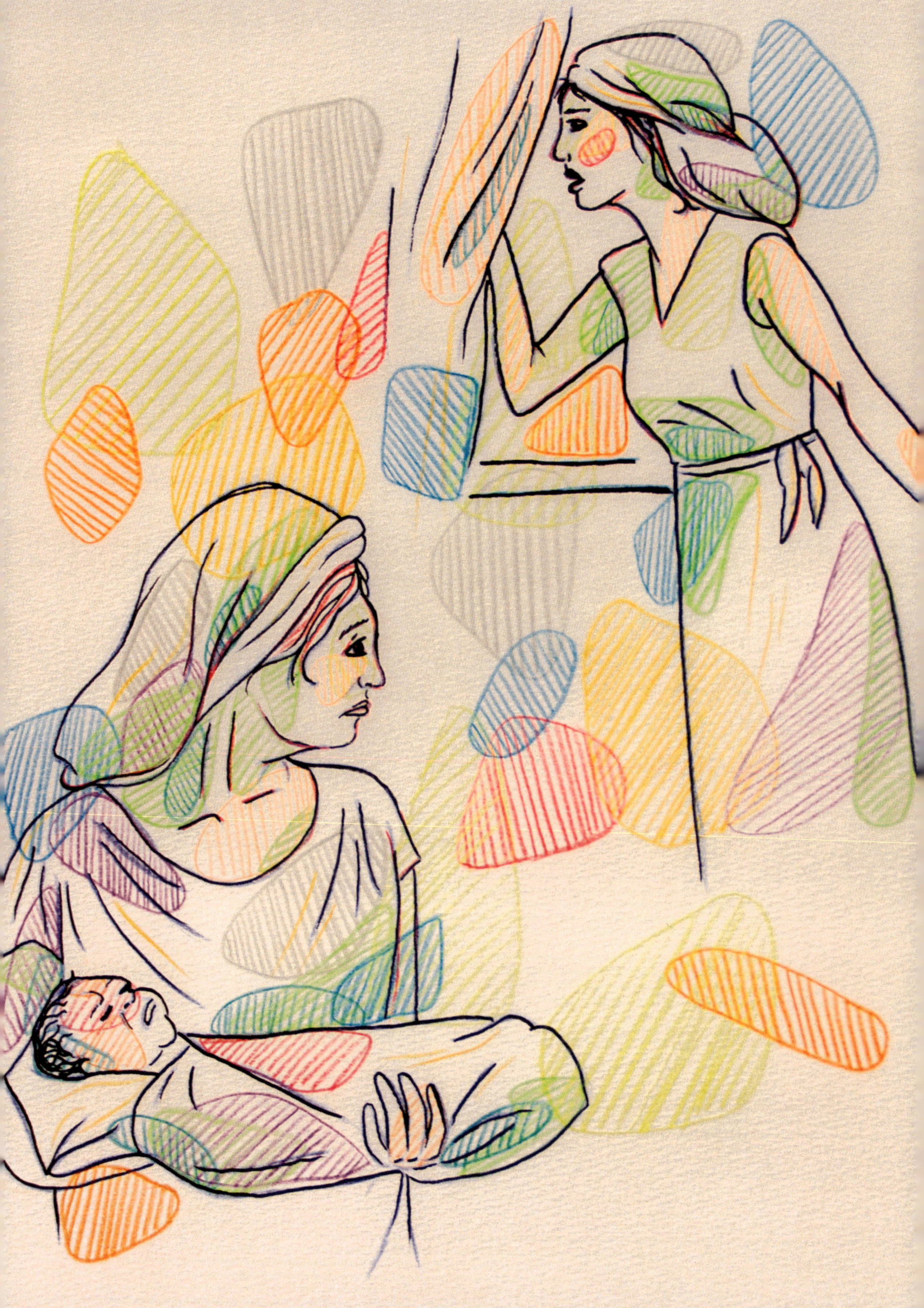

Jochebed

Her baby's cries were impossible to stop. Jochebed tried to calm him and keep him quiet. If Pharaoh's soldiers found out that there was a baby in the house, they would come for him and take him away. The pharaoh of Egypt, the country where Jochebed's family lived, had ordered that all the children of the Jews be thrown into the river as soon as they were born. For the last three months since her little boy was born, Jochebed had tried to hide him at all costs. No one should hear him. No one should see him. No one should know of his existence.

She fed him even before he was hungry, constantly checking his diaper, making sure he didn't need anything. All to avoid him crying. Fear overwhelmed her every time her baby whimpered. She would wake up in the middle of the night, fearing someone else would hear him. How could her little boy understand that he had to keep quiet? It was getting harder and harder. She couldn't hide him much longer.

God had to do something. Jochebed didn't understand what was happening. Pharaoh hated the Hebrews. But God was on their side. Why didn't He make Pharaoh change his mind? Why did this law not cease to exist? God was more powerful than Pharaoh; why had He allowed this to happen?

She finally had to do it. She put her baby in a basket she had prepared to keep out the water. She left the house with it in her arms and placed it on the riverbank. She watched with tear-filled eyes as the river's current carried her little boy away.

"Oh, God, take care of this child for me."

God took care of him. Pharaoh's daughter found the basket and the child crying inside. She decided to keep him, but she wanted someone else to care for him, and Jochebed did. Jochebed took her son in her arms again and hugged and kissed him again. She could finally sing lullabies to him without fear of being overheard. She was able to cradle him in her arms during the day. She was able to watch him grow and teach him. There was so much she wanted to show him. God had heard her prayer. He had saved her little boy from the river. Jochebed thus learned that she could trust Him and be obedient despite difficulties and not understanding why things happen.

Exodus 2:1-10; 6:20

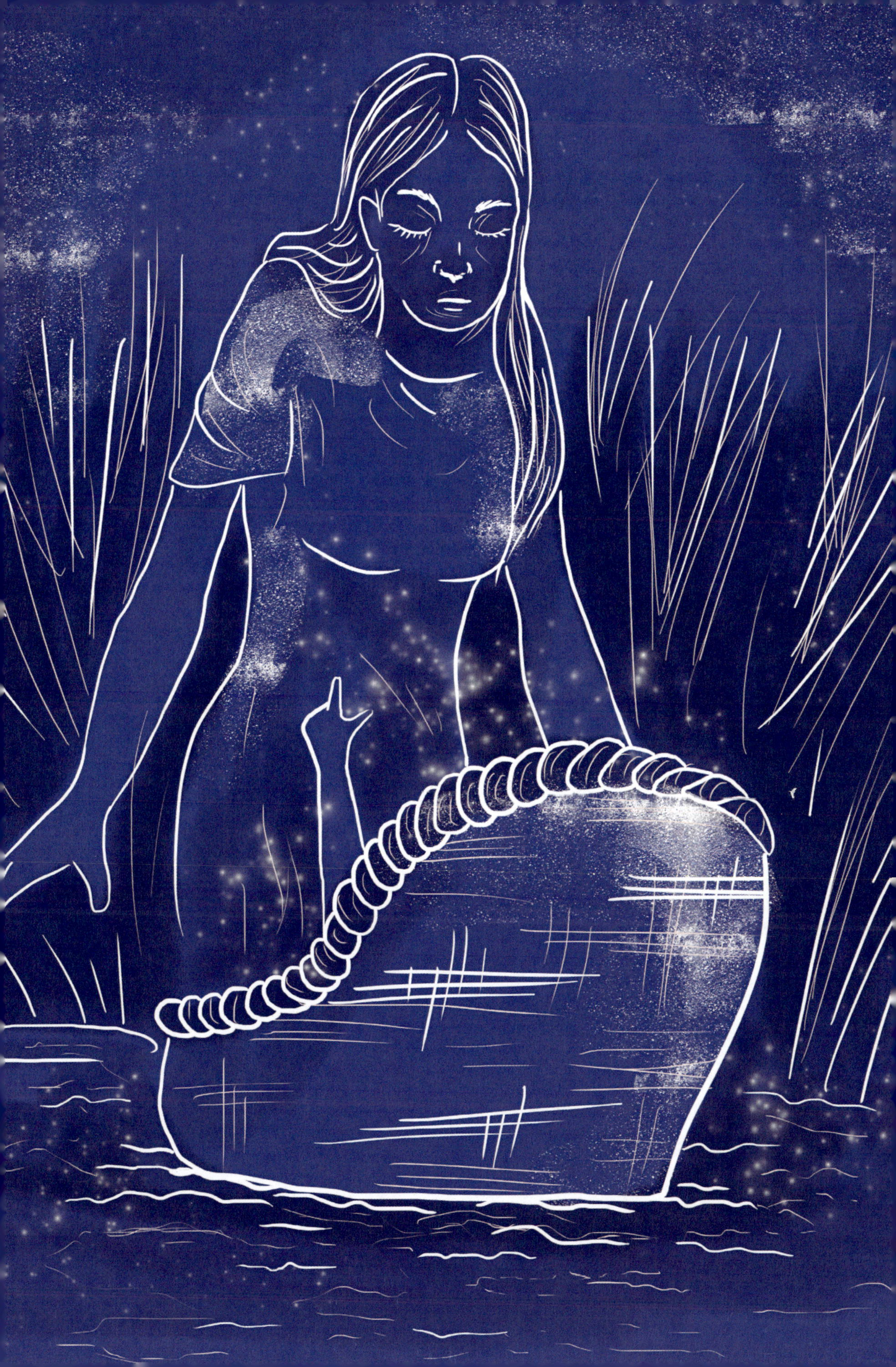

Miriam

Little Miriam, while watching over her brother's basket floating on the Nile River, could've never imagined that this months-old baby in danger of drowning would one day become the liberator of God's people, slaves in the land of Egypt. She would've never thought, seeing Pharaoh's daughter find him and pull him out of the water, that 80 years later, this boy would come back to confront Pharaoh's household. It would've been impossible for her to imagine when she offered herself to find a woman to take care of the baby for the princess, that she, accompanied by her two brothers, would lead the rest of the Israelites through the desert to a new land that God had promised to give them.

But that's what actually happened. Miriam, along with her brothers Moses and Aaron, witnessed the power of God and His love for His people, whom He rescued from a life of slavery and continuous suffering. That day, Miriam saw how the abundant waters of the sea parted, opening a way for God's people to cross. The fear was indescribable, not only because of the miracle their eyes were seeing, but also because of the speed with which the Egyptians advanced, chasing them in their chariots, ready to put an end to their lives. But suddenly, when all the Israelites reached the other shore, the sea waters returned to their place, covering the Egyptians, along with their chariots and horses.

"Sing to the Lord! Because He has done wonderful things. He put an end to those who persecuted us," Miriam shouted with a tambourine in her hand. Then a crowd of women began to sing and dance with her, worshiping God.

Miriam was not always an exemplary woman and a good leader. On certain occasions, she also made mistakes. Once she and Aaron criticized Moses and his wife. Miriam was punished and had a few very difficult days that made her think about what had happened. Miriam was very sorry. God saw her heart and forgave her. He didn't allow the people continue their journey until she was also ready to go with them. Not many women had the opportunity to be leaders in times like those; without a doubt, Miriam was a remarkable woman.

Exodus 1:1-10; 15:20-21,
Numbers 12:1-15,
Micah 6:4

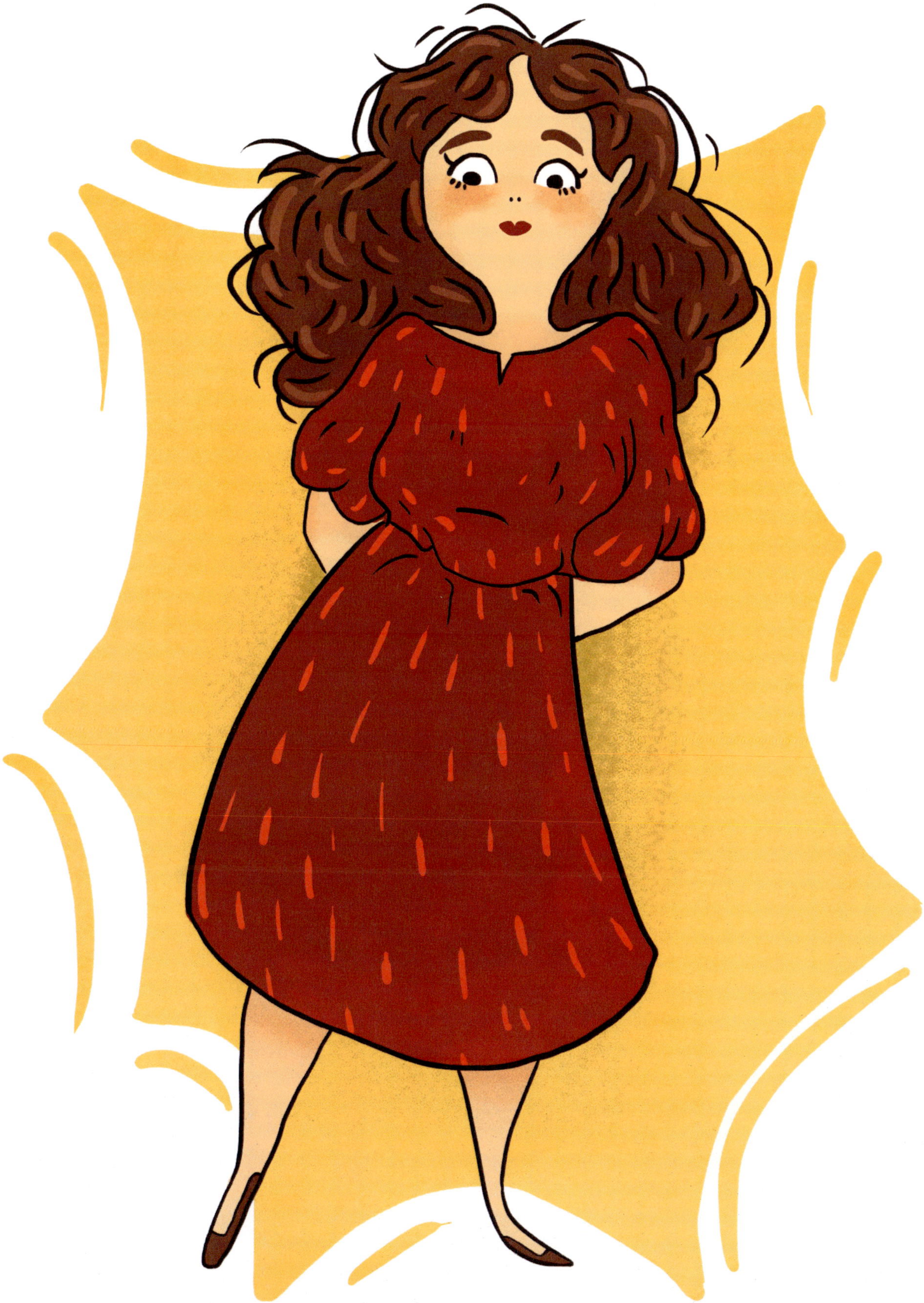

Zipporah

Zipporah met Moses under unusual circumstances. One day with her sisters, she was drawing water from the well to give the family's sheep a drink when some shepherds drove them away. Moses, watching everything from afar, approached and defended them. Although it might not have seemed like it, he was a man full of fears and insecurities; he had come to Midian, fleeing from Egypt, where Pharaoh wanted to kill him.

A short time passed before Zipporah and Moses married, started a family, and had two children. During these years, God worked in their lives and prepared them for what was to come: a special mission.

One day, Moses returned home speaking of a bush on fire that would not burn up and through which he had received orders from God. It was hard for Zipporah to believe. However, during all these years, Zipporah had heard much about the God of the Israelites. Moses had shared the stories of his people with her, although by now, they were distant stories for him. Now, Moses had received the mission to go face the pharaoh of Egypt and free God's people from slavery. He felt very insecure about it; it seemed impossible to achieve. Zipporah was determined to go with him and support him in this mission.

It was not easy for Zipporah to leave her land and her family to go defend an exploited and mistreated people for whom the possibilities of freedom seemed limited. Zipporah didn't know how the Israelites would receive her. After all, she wasn't one of them; she was a foreigner who had never suffered what they suffered. But Zipporah, seeing Moses' confidence that God would do what He said, was determined to go with him.

The disputes with Pharaoh became tense, and the danger increased. God showed His power in unimaginable ways. Finally, God gave victory to His people, and the Israelites left Egypt, led by Moses. Zipporah had the privilege of enjoying the freedom of the Israelites with the rest of the people.

Exodus 2:16-22; 4:18-26; 18:1-6

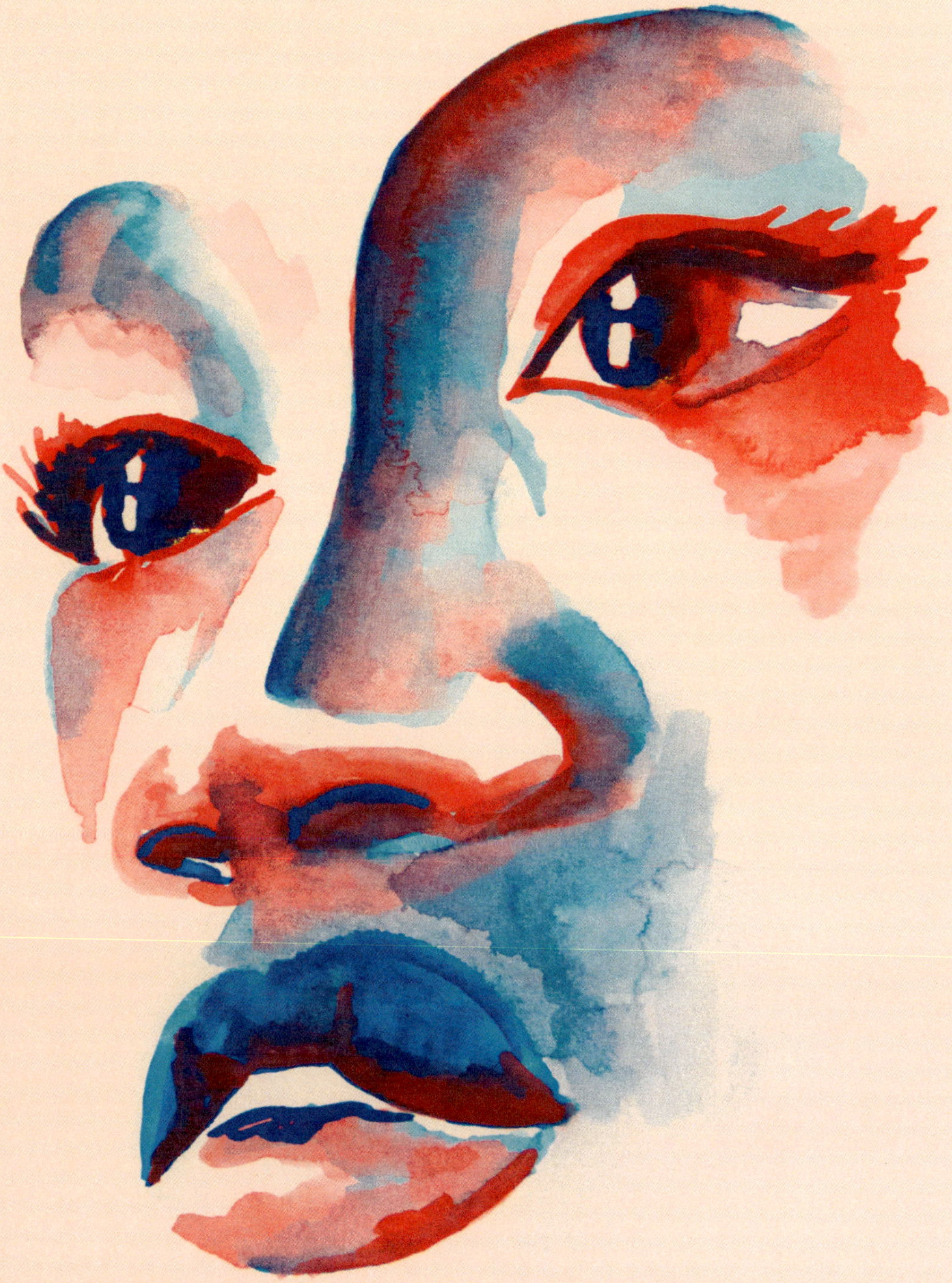

Elisheba

It was an exciting day for everyone. After months of gathering materials and building, they were finally celebrating the dedication of the tabernacle. God had ordered the construction of this mobile tent where He Himself would dwell and accompany them throughout their journey through the desert on their search for the long-awaited Promised Land. The last year and a half since her brother-in-law had come to Aaron, her husband, to tell him what God was calling them to do had been very intense. Elisheba had waited nervously every time her husband went with Moses to see Pharaoh to ask him to let them go. She had worked hard to convince the people to trust her brother-in-law, Moses, whom God had chosen as their leader. She had watched with amazement not only the plagues in Egypt but also how the waters of the sea parted, and she had wept as she crossed on dry land. And today, once again, her eyes teared up upon seeing the place that God had prepared to walk with them finally finished.

Just then, Elisheba saw her brother Nahshon, the military leader of Judah, walk solemnly forward. The giving of the tabernacle dedication offerings had just begun. Elisheba looked at her son Ithamar, who was also there. That gleam in his eyes said everything. Ithamar had worked tirelessly to ensure they had all the necessary materials to build the tabernacle. How proud she was of him. Standing beside her, her husband Aaron kept his eyes fixed on the ceremony taking place before them. Aaron had also worked so hard to make all this possible. This building would become a very important place for her family from that moment on. As the high priest, Aaron would be the only one allowed to enter the tabernacle's interior to represent all the people. It was a very privileged role that his son Eleazar would have after him, and later his grandson Phinehas, and his descendants would continue for many years of Israel's history.

Elisheba's heart was pounding. So much work, so much effort, so many past nerves and fears. It was worth seeing how God Himself took His place among His people.

Exodus 6:23

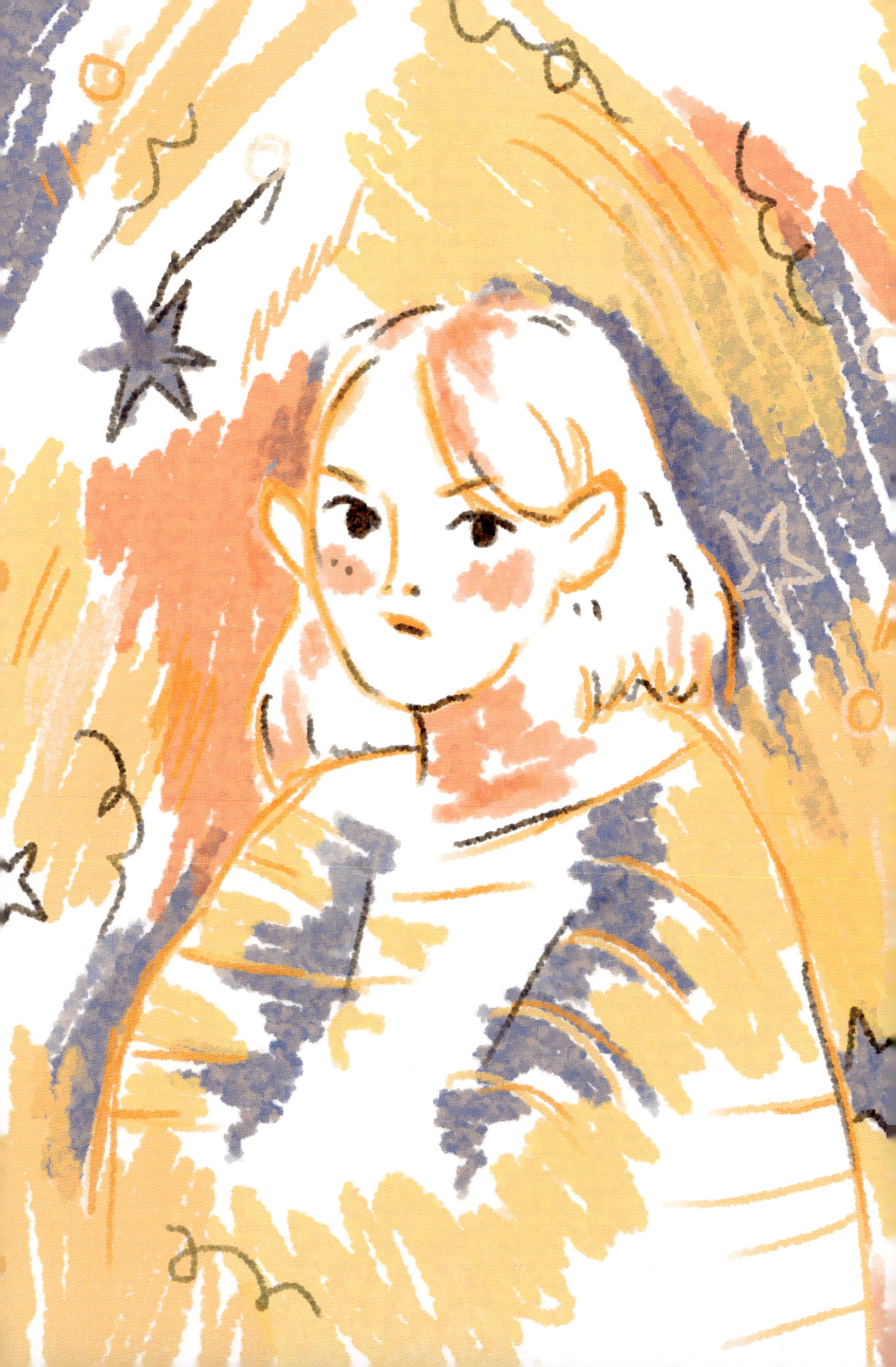

Mahlah, Noah, Hoglah, Milkah and Tirzah

For 40 years, the people of Israel wandered through the desert waiting to receive the Promised Land, a place God had prepared for His own people. Among the many families that lived in the desert was Zelophehad, who had five daughters. Years passed, and their father died, leaving Mahlah, Noah, Hoglah, Milkah, and Tirzah alone. Finally, the Israelites reached the land that God had promised them.

Shortly before finally inhabiting the land, Moses, who had been given the job of leading the Israelites, began the complicated task of dividing the territory among all the Israelites. At that time, women didn't have many privileges, so following the laws of the time, Moses' plan only included distributing the land among the men. Most of the women of Israel would receive a place to live since they would live with their fathers, husbands, sons... But there were no men with whom Mahlah, Noah, Hoglah, Milkah, and Tirzah could live. In their family, there were only women.

"Where will we live? It's not fair for us to not receive anything just because we're women. We should go talk to Moses," commented one of the sisters.

And that's what they did. At the time, surely, many would think this was crazy. How could some women have a land of their own?

Of course, God understood the need of these five sisters and wouldn't allow them to not have a part in the place He had prepared for all His people, men and women alike. God made Moses understand that the five sisters had just as much right as any other man and made him see the unjust laws that didn't allow this to happen.

Thanks to their courage, Mahlah, Noah, Hoglah, Milkah, and Tirzah also received a place to live, like the rest of the Israelites. But also, because they raised their voices, the law was changed that very day, and from then on, other women in the same situation would also enjoy that privilege.

Numbers 27:1-11

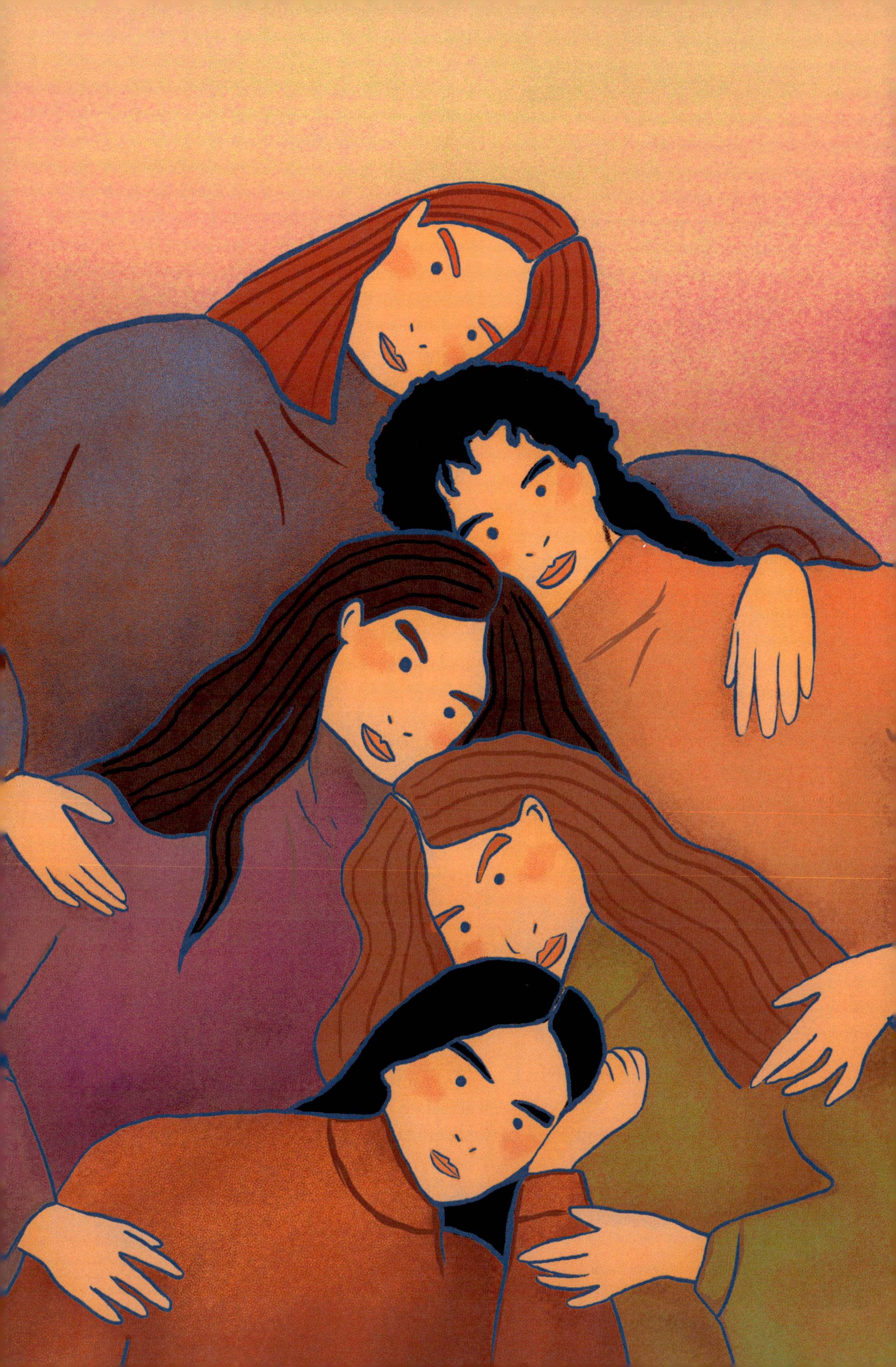

Rahab

The city of Jericho, where Rahab lived, was in total turmoil in those days. There was no talk of anything other than a dangerously approaching nation. Rahab had heard thousands of stories about the Israelites and their God: rivers turned to blood, locust invasions, hailstorms, and days without sunlight. This same God had also parted the waters of the sea so His people could walk across it. Rahab also heard about the terrible things that had happened to the Pharaoh of Egypt himself and to the kings of nearby nations, all for opposing the God of the people of Israel. A God who, as many claimed to have seen, constantly accompanied His people in the form of a huge pillar of cloud during the day and of fire at night.

Rahab knew Jericho was difficult to conquer because a great wall protected it. There, right on the wall, was her house. Rahab couldn't stop looking out her window, where she could see the other side, hoping to see some miracle indicating that the God of the Israelites was getting close.

One day, two men came to her house. Although they tried to hide it, Rahab knew they were Israelites. She got very scared. She didn't think their God would like the kind of life she lived. The king of Jericho heard about the spies and began to look for them. Rahab hid them in her house and told the king they had left. She then helped them to escape through the window when no one was watching.

"I believe in God and know He is God of gods both in heaven and on earth. Please save my life and my family's," she told the two men.

Rahab tied a red rope to the window. That rope served as a sign on the day of the conquest, and God protected everyone who was in the house.

Rahab became one more among the Israelites. She changed her life, married, started a family, and had children, grandchildren, and great-grandchildren. From her offspring came Jesus, who would save both Israelites and non-Israelites. We also remember her as one of the heroines of the faith for her great trust in God, even when nothing seemed to indicate that she could be part of this special people.

Joshua 2:1-24; 6:22-25,
Hebrews 11:31

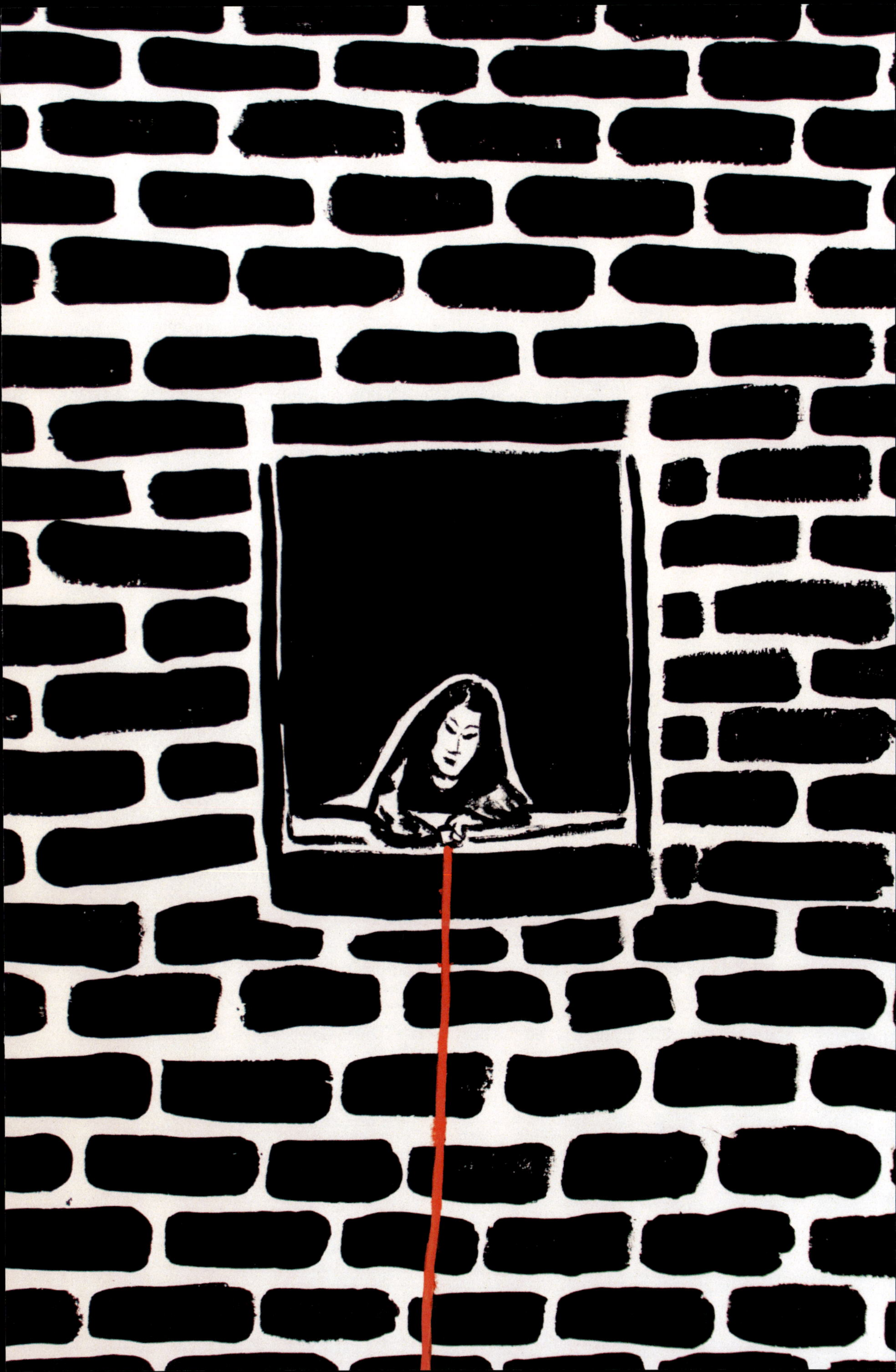

Aksah

Aksah remembered her wedding day. These were times of many changes for the Israelites. Little by little, they began settling in their longed-for land, the one God had promised them. Her father, Caleb, had steadfastly fought for it. Aksah had heard him talk incessantly about God's goodness, care, and protection. She was his only child, his special little girl. Caleb wanted to make sure she had a good husband. Othniel had just returned from conquering the city of Debir, and he seemed brave, determined, and faithful to God. Yes, Othniel would definitely make a good husband for Aksah.

As a wedding gift, Othniel and Aksah received a piece of land. Othniel toured the territory and returned to tell Aksah everything he had seen. It was a large enough piece of land; they both imagined how happy they would be there. Only one thing worried Othniel: it was a semi-desert area, and it would not be easy to grow crops. That could make it difficult to feed their family. They would need some additional land. Othniel thought it would be a good idea if Aksah talked to her father and asked him to increase their land. Aksah thought about it. More land would be a great idea, but she came up with something even better. She immediately went to visit her father. Actually, what they lacked wasn't land. They had enough land; they just needed water, springs of water.

As Caleb listened to his daughter, looking at her, he recognized himself some years ago when he and 11 other Israelites visited the land they were now dividing up. Now, all that seemed very far away. They were very difficult cities to conquer, but it was a wonderful place. God had found a perfect place for them. The others thought it would be best to find another land, even if it wasn't as good. But he and his friend Joshua saw it clearly. They wanted the best and knew that God would help them achieve it. Aksah looked a lot like him. She was smart, brave, and wanted the best for her family. Caleb smiled at his daughter and expanded her fields. They would no longer own just the initial land; their territory would also include an area full of springs to the north and another with more springs to the south. Aksah smiled too.

Joshua 15:16-19,
Judges 1:12-15

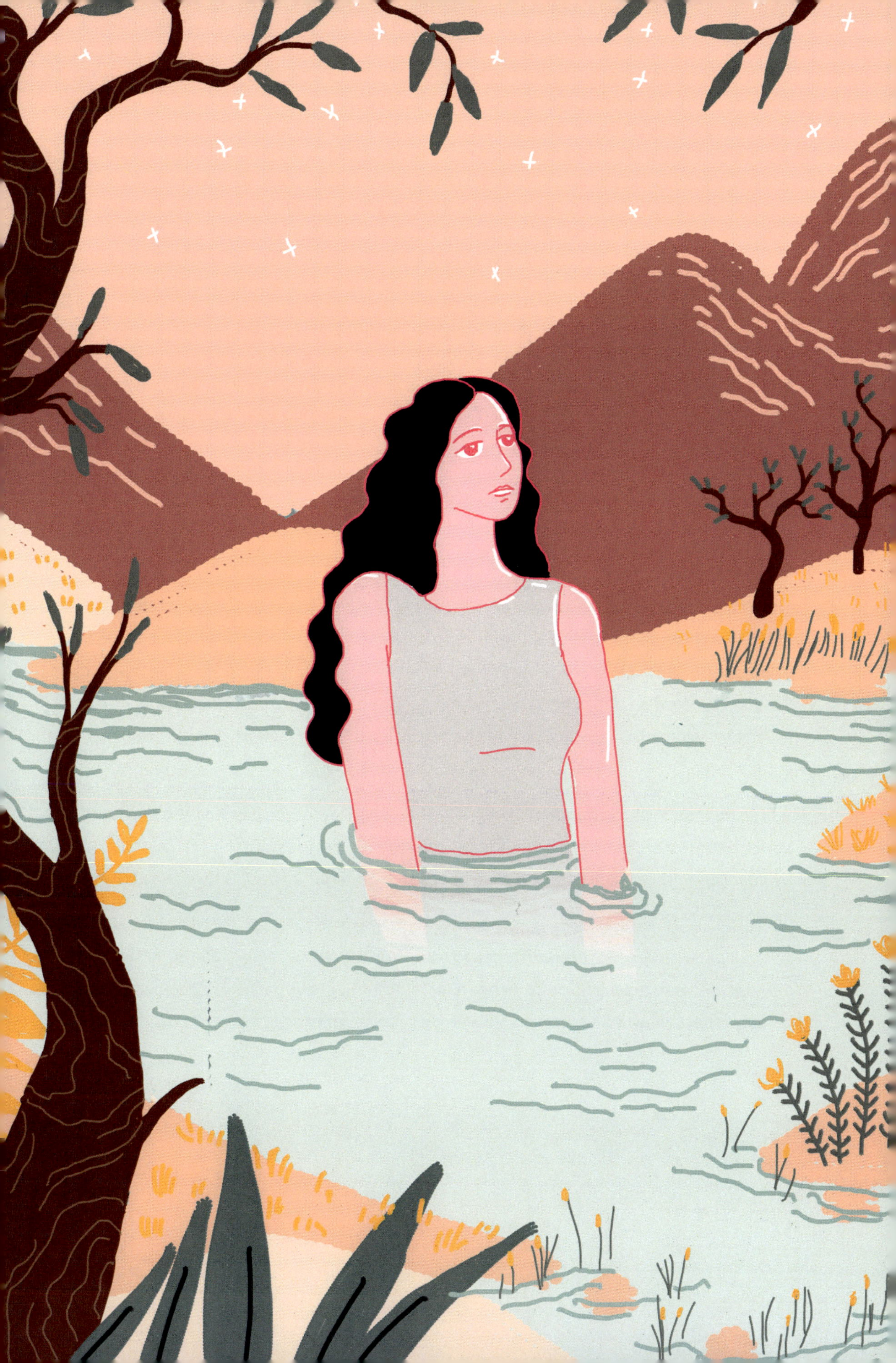

Sheerah

Sheerah walked confidently through the streets of Upper Beth-Horon. As she did so, she observed the houses where their inhabitants lived their day-to-day lives, with their joys and their difficulties, their hopes and their fears. Some of the neighbors had already gotten up and started their workday. They smiled at her when they saw her go by. Everyone in Beth-Horon knew Sheerah, and everyone was grateful to that strong and brave woman, unlike many others — the founder of their city.

It was a small city, although later it would grow. It was impossible for Sheerah to imagine that, in the future, Solomon, the wisest of the kings of Israel, would make it great and put a strong wall around it to protect it. It was a city located at a strategic point.

Sheerah passed the last house on the outskirts of the city. She especially liked this place. From here, high above, she could see the road leading down from the mountains to the valley and how the land spread everywhere. That's what had once made her fall in love with the place. She sat on a rock and watched the sunbeams break through the dawn. Little by little, they colored the land Joshua had given to Ephraim, her grandfather, so his tribe could settle there.

A little further down, on another nearby hill, Sheerah saw that the day was also starting at Lower Beth-Horon. She, too, had built that other city. There was still a third city established by her, though she couldn't see it from there, Uzzen-Sheerah, a special city she had named after herself.

As she looked at the scenery and listened to how life in the city became active on yet another morning, Sheerah thanked God in her heart for allowing her to be part of His people's history in such a special way. What an enormous privilege to be a blessing to others!

1 Chronicles 7:24

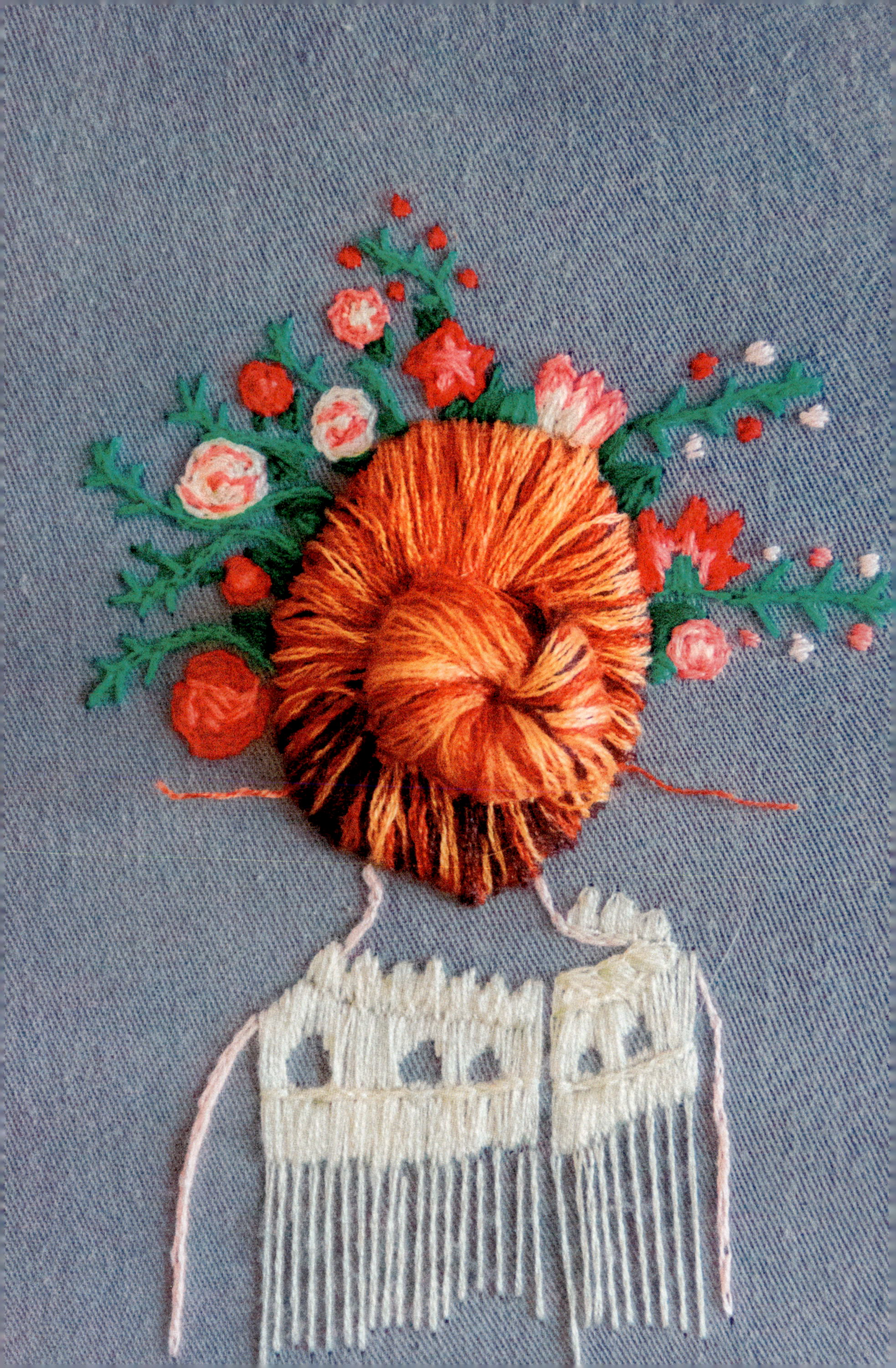

Deborah

Before kings ruled Israel, God chose leaders who led His nation, one of whom was Deborah. In addition to being a ruler of Israel, she was a prophetess; God spoke through her.

Every morning, Deborah sat in the shade of a well-known palm tree on top of a hill, where people came to present their problems and disputes before her. Deborah dispensed justice and made sure that the nation was at peace. But Israel had no peace with neighboring nations. Specifically, a Canaanite army had been terrorizing the Israelites for the past 20 years.

One day, God told Deborah to encourage an Israelite named Barak to raise an army and go fight the Canaanites. Barak didn't feel very safe because the Canaanites had a large army, and the Israelites were very afraid of them. He told Deborah that he would only go to battle if she accompanied them. At that time, battles were just a man's thing — no women were trained to fight — but Deborah trusted God and was sure they would win, so she accepted and enlisted with the rest of the army.

The day of the battle arrived, and Deborah went to Barak and said: "Let's go, Barak! Today is a day of victory. God goes before us; we have nothing to fear."

The Israelite army defeated the Canaanites on that day, and Israel remained at peace for the next 40 years. Since then, Deborah has been acclaimed and remembered as the mother of Israel. She is also the author of one of the oldest songs recorder in Bibles.

Judges 4-5

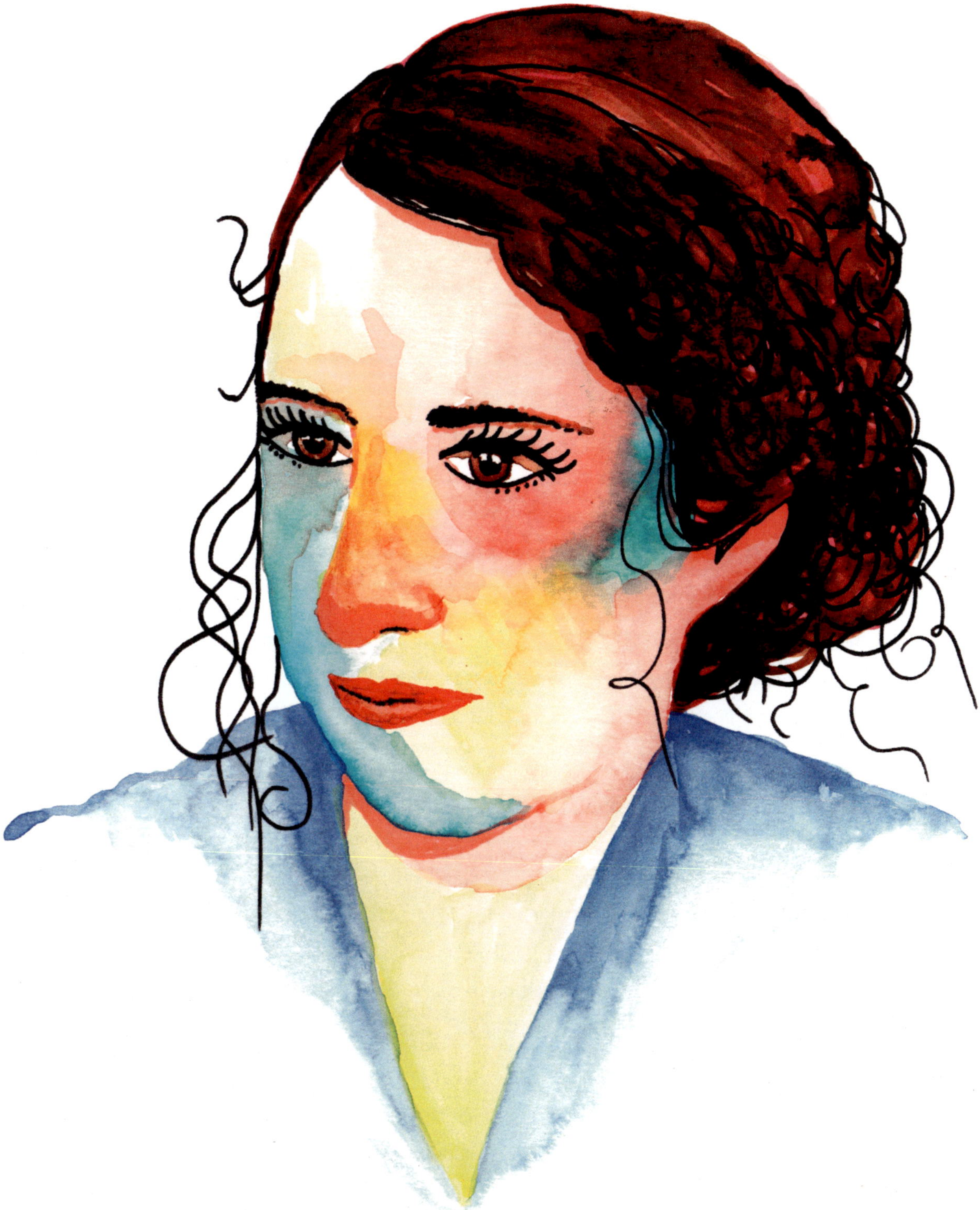

Jael

Jael was in her shop putting away the work tools she used to beat and shape iron. She thought about everything that was happening around her that day. As her husband had told her, the Israelites had finally decided to attack the Canaanites after so many years. It was hard to believe!

Suddenly, Jael heard something outside her tent. She looked out and saw a man hunkered down. Perhaps one of the men in the battle had escaped and was badly wounded. She wasn't quite sure what to do. Her husband had always insisted that remaining on the sidelines of warring nations was best. The most convenient thing was not to go for or against any other nation. She looked closer; there was no doubt that the man was Sisera, the head of the Canaanite army. Neither their iron chariots nor their troops seemed to have been able to defeat the Israelites.

Sisera went up to Jael and asked her for water. Jael's whole body trembled. She let Sisera come into her tent and gave him some milk. Sisera gulped it down, leaned back for a moment, and fell asleep immediately. He was exhausted.

There he was, right beside Jael, one of the most powerful men in the region. Everybody would be looking for him. If only they knew he was there, covered in bruises and asleep in her tent. Of course, nobody would imagine that he was hidden there with her. Actually, she hadn't decided to protect him, he just came, and she had no choice. Was she helping the head of an oppressive nation? Which side was she on? Of course, her husband would've told her a thousand times not to get involved in other people's battles. But her husband wasn't there now. And Jael had a decision to make. She liked the Israelites. Besides, she knew something about their God. She wouldn't oppose God; she preferred to be against the Canaanites.

So, Jael grabbed an iron bar and, without much thought, put an end to the last member of the Canaanite army. Jael didn't know it, but just a few hours before, Deborah, the leader of Israel, had prophesied that God would deliver the Canaanites into the hands of a woman. Although Jael was unaware of it, God had used her, a simple Kenite blacksmith, to bring victory to His people.

Judges 4:17-23

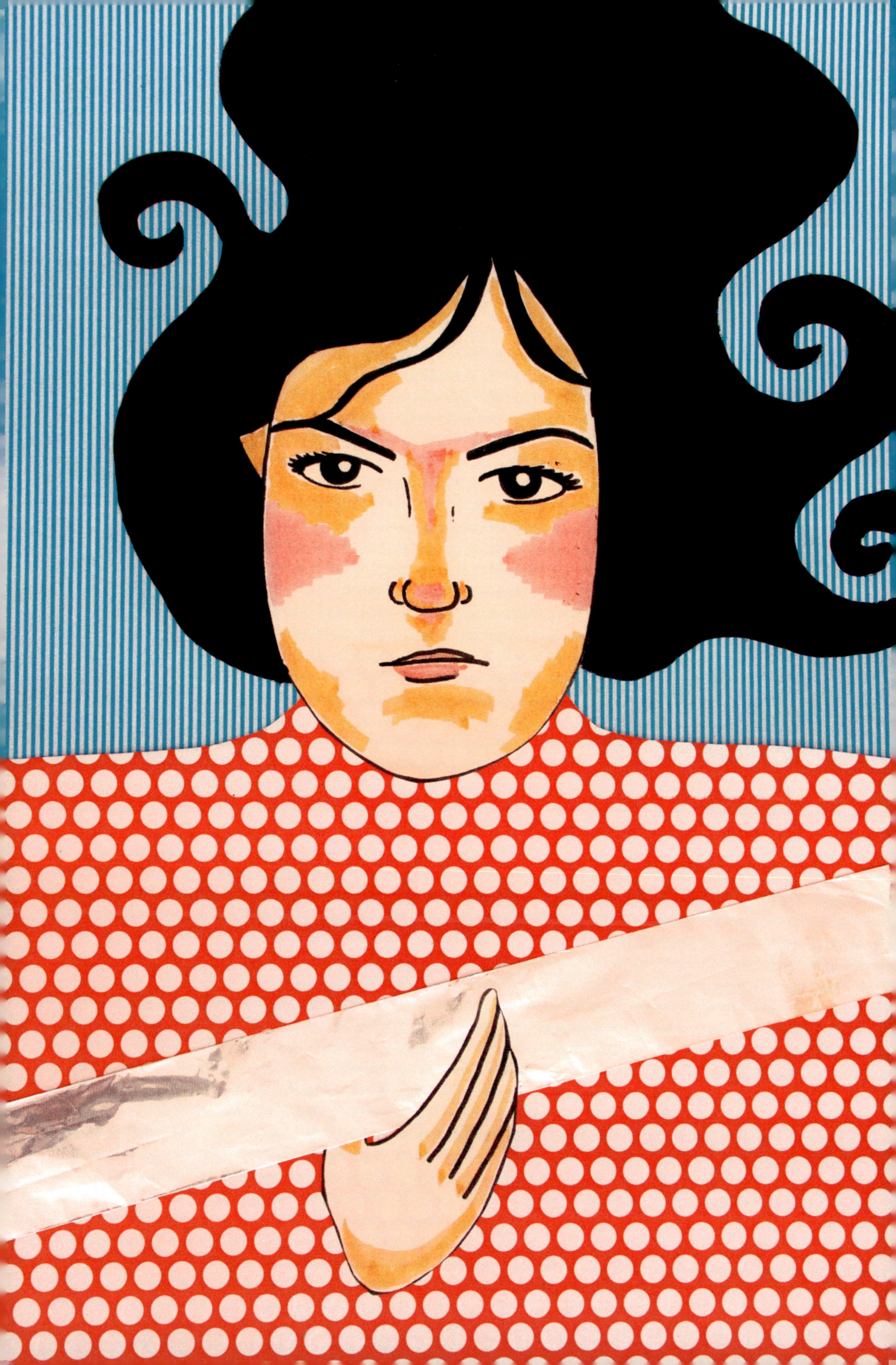

Naomi

Naomi lived in Bethlehem with her husband and two children. Those times were very difficult because both work and food were scarce. For this reason, her family decided to take a very long trip and look for a new place to live. They decided to go to Moab. There weren't many Jews in Moab; the people there barely knew about God. But, despite the difficulty of starting a life in another country, Naomi had many hopes and dreams for this new stage in her life.

They settled into their new home and adapted little by little. Her husband started working, and her children married and began their own families. Everything seemed to be going well until something horrible happened. Naomi's husband suddenly died.

Naomi felt very sad. It was very difficult for her to be in a country that wasn't hers, and even more so without her husband. Women at that time didn't work. So, if they had no husband, they had no money. They had nothing, not even anything to eat. Luckily, Naomi had two children who took care of her.

But the sad things didn't end there. Shortly after that, one of her sons died. And then Naomi's other son died as well.

Naomi was totally heartbroken. She felt really sad. Now she had nothing. And at her age! She was alone in a country that wasn't hers. She decided to go back to Bethlehem, where maybe someone could help her. And she left crying, thinking about changing her name. From then on, she would be called Mara, which means "bitterness."

But God still saw the same sweet woman she had always been, and He wasn't going to leave her alone. Ruth, the woman who had married one of her sons, was watching her; she worried a lot about Naomi, so she decided to go with her. When they arrived in Bethlehem, God had prepared everything for them. The famine was over, and there was enough food and work. He also provided other people who helped them. God took care of every detail. Naomi never thought of calling herself Mara again. God blessed her life with Ruth and her new family.

Ruth 1-4

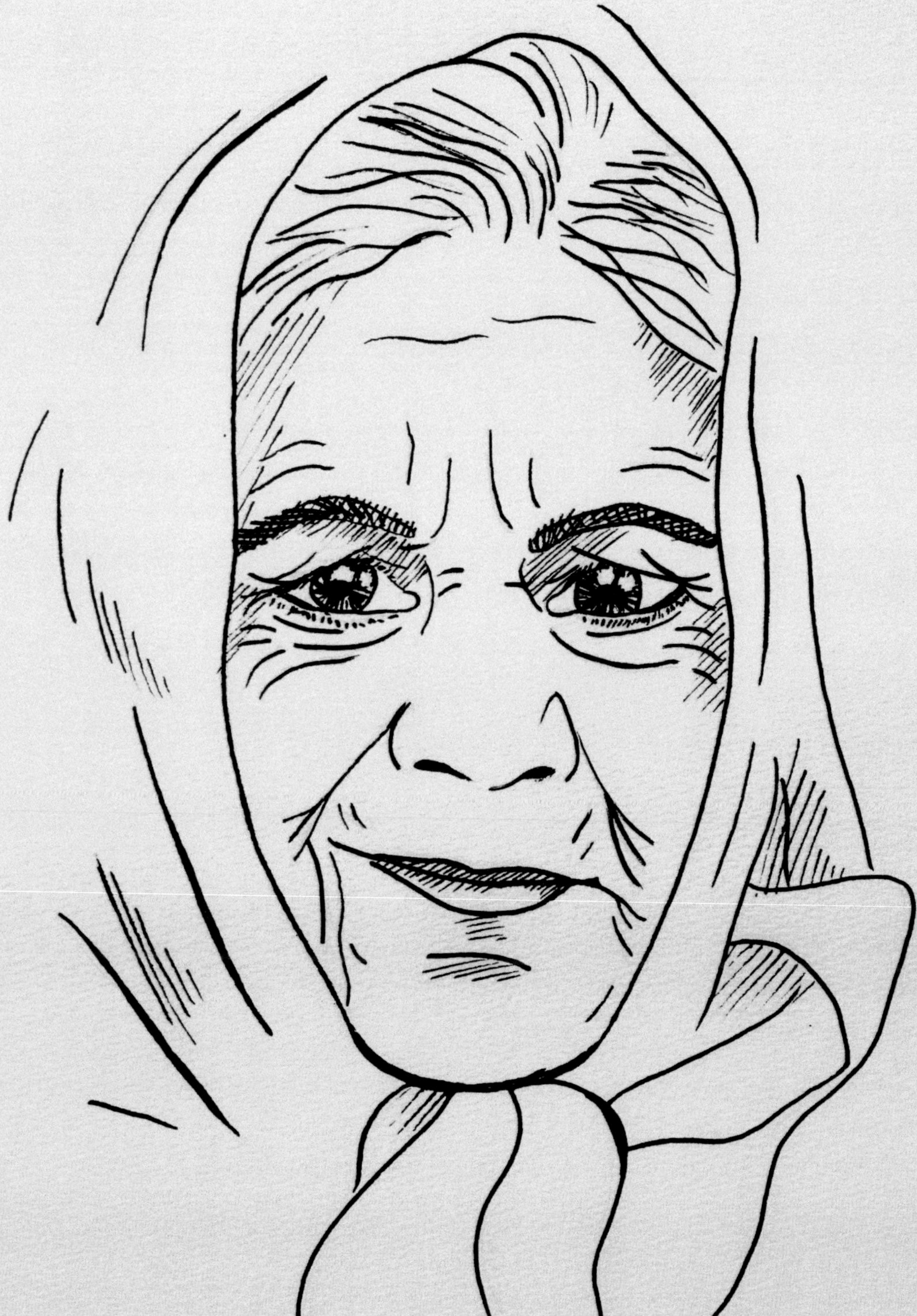

Ruth

Ruth was born in Moab. The people of Moab didn't know about God, so Ruth had never heard of Him. But one day, a Jewish family came to her country. It was Naomi's family. Ruth met one of Naomi's sons and married him. Naomi's family spoke to Ruth about God; Ruth believed in God.

But some after, something very sad happened in her family. First, her father-in-law died, and then her brother-in-law, and even her own husband died as well. Ruth was suddenly a widow. This caused her immense pain. Sadness overwhelmed her as she tried to think about her future; surely, returning to her parents' house was her best option. However, despite her own pain, she could see her mother-in-law's deep sadness. Naomi was helpless. She believed that she would never get over the loss of her husband and children. She thought that she would be alone forever from then on, but Ruth was there to help.

"You should leave and look for another husband because if not, you will be left alone like me," Naomi told Ruth.

Ruth, who was very worried about her, said: "Wherever you go, I'll go, your people will be my people, and your God will also become my God. I'm not going to leave you alone."

So, Naomi went back to her city. Ruth left her homeland, friends, family, and everything she had there and went with Naomi.

Each day, Ruth would visit the barley fields after the workers had harvested all the grain, picking up the stalks that had fallen and taking them home to make flour and bread for the two of them to eat.

From then on, Ruth always lived with Naomi. Ruth later remarried. So she went to live in her husband's house and took Naomi with her. When Ruth had a son, Naomi took care of him as his grandmother. This son, Obed, would be one of the ancestors of Jesus.

Ruth 1-4

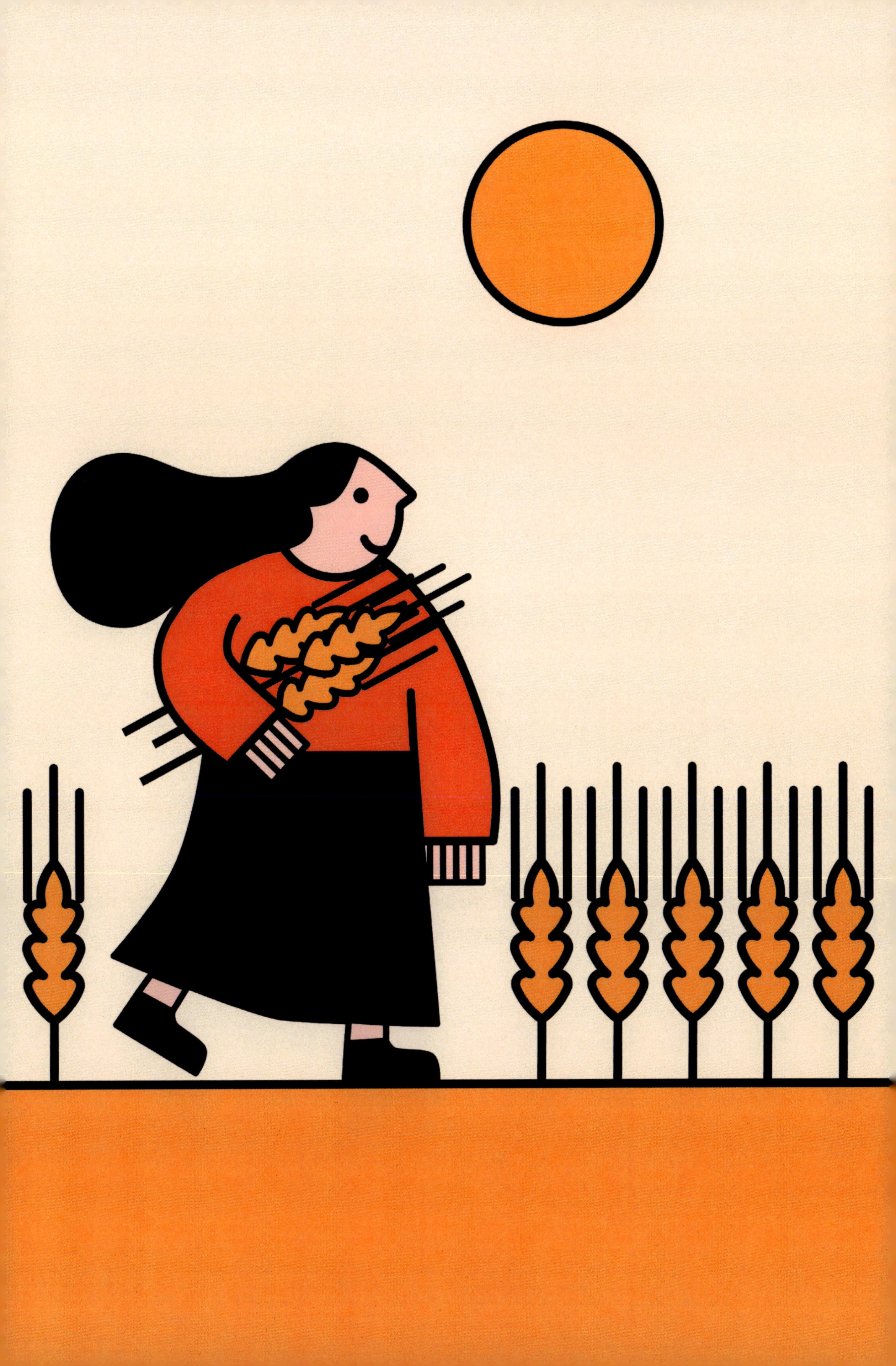

Hannah

The sadness that Hannah experienced was very deep. She felt lonely and empty. Something in her life caused her constant pain: Hannah had no children. All the women around her were mothers; she wished she could be one, too. She thought the others looked at her with pity. Hannah imagined them making fun of her behind her back. She felt ashamed. It was her greatest wish: she had dreamed of a baby since she was very young, but it seemed it would never come true. Hannah couldn't stop thinking about it. She couldn't sleep at night and could barely eat.

During a family trip, in a moment of desperation, Hannah went to the sanctuary to pray. In her silence and loneliness, she fell on her face before God and began to cry and ask Him to comfort her heart. Soundless words came out of her mouth and mixed with the tears that flowed from her restless eyes. Until then, no one else could make Hannah feel better, no matter how hard they tried to cheer her up. The suffering she was going through was difficult for others to understand. Hannah poured her heart out before God. Little by little, she let God take away her pain and fill her heart with peace and comfort. There, Hannah finally felt understood.

After praying for a while, Hannah got up and felt motivated enough to continue living. Her time with God allowed her to recover her strength, and she was able to eat again. The heavy burden of sadness became lighter and even bearable. That afternoon, Hannah returned with a smile, even though she was still sad that she didn't have a child. She knew she wasn't alone. She knew she was loved and understood. She had discovered the joy of God.

Hannah would cry in that place once again just a few years later — this time with her baby, Samuel, in her arms. But now, her tears were tears of joy. Joy for a heart that found the hope it had lost in God. The child she had felt growing within her belonged to God, and she gave him to God.

1 Samuel 1:1-2:10

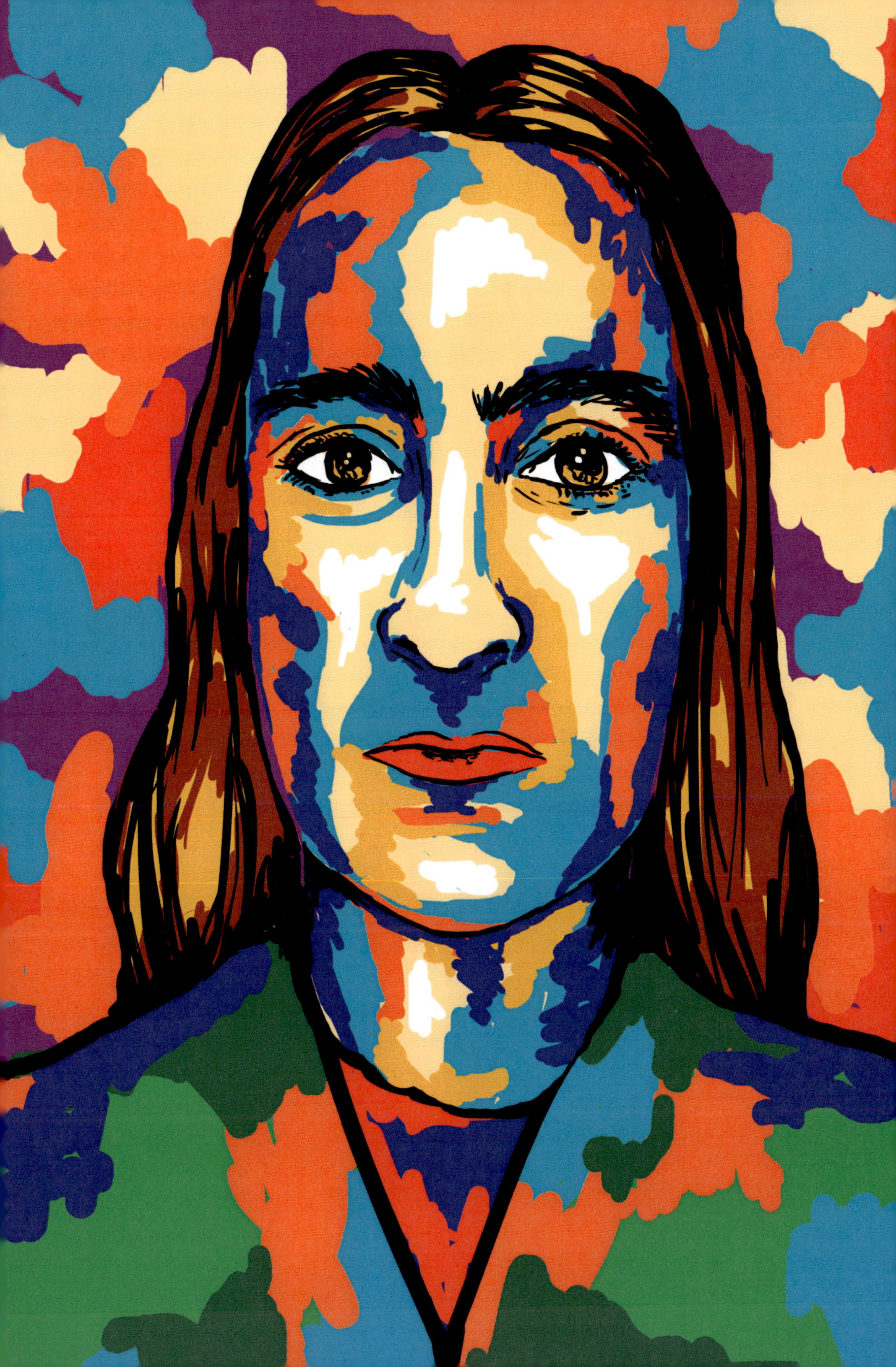

Ahinoam

Just as she did every morning, Ahinoam took a moment to sit in her favorite spot. The house seemed empty; there was no trace of her husband and their six children. She remembered when they were little; the house had always seemed full and noisy. Now, grown up, they had their own lives. A melancholy shiver ran through Ahinoam's stomach; how she missed those past years!

Ahinoam met Saul some time ago. That tall, brave, dark, handsome man had caught her eye from the beginning. They got married, and then the children came. Together they raised them in the God's love and knowledge of the law. Their four sons — Jonathan, Abinadab, Malchuishua, and Ishbosheth — and their two daughters, Merab and Michal, learned from an early age what it meant to be part of God's people.

It was a true honor for Ahinoam to learn that Saul had been chosen as king of Israel. She knew it was a great responsibility for her entire family, but serving God's people was a great privilege. Being the king of Israel was a difficult task; over the years, its burden became heavier and heavier. Greater difficulties and harder responsibilities came. Ahinoam saw how her husband gradually became someone different and moved away from the figure of that exemplary king that everyone believed he would be.

She couldn't help but think of her children. She had done her part and taught them the best she could. Now they were adults and had their own lives; it was up to them to make their own decisions. Sometimes their choices were good; other times, they made serious mistakes. Some started well, and then something tripped them up. Ahinoam rejoiced at their victories and suffered over each of their failures as she wondered if she had done her job well. Sometimes she doubted herself. But she had already done her part: raising her children in the love of God. What an adventure and a great privilege!

1 Samuel 14:49-50

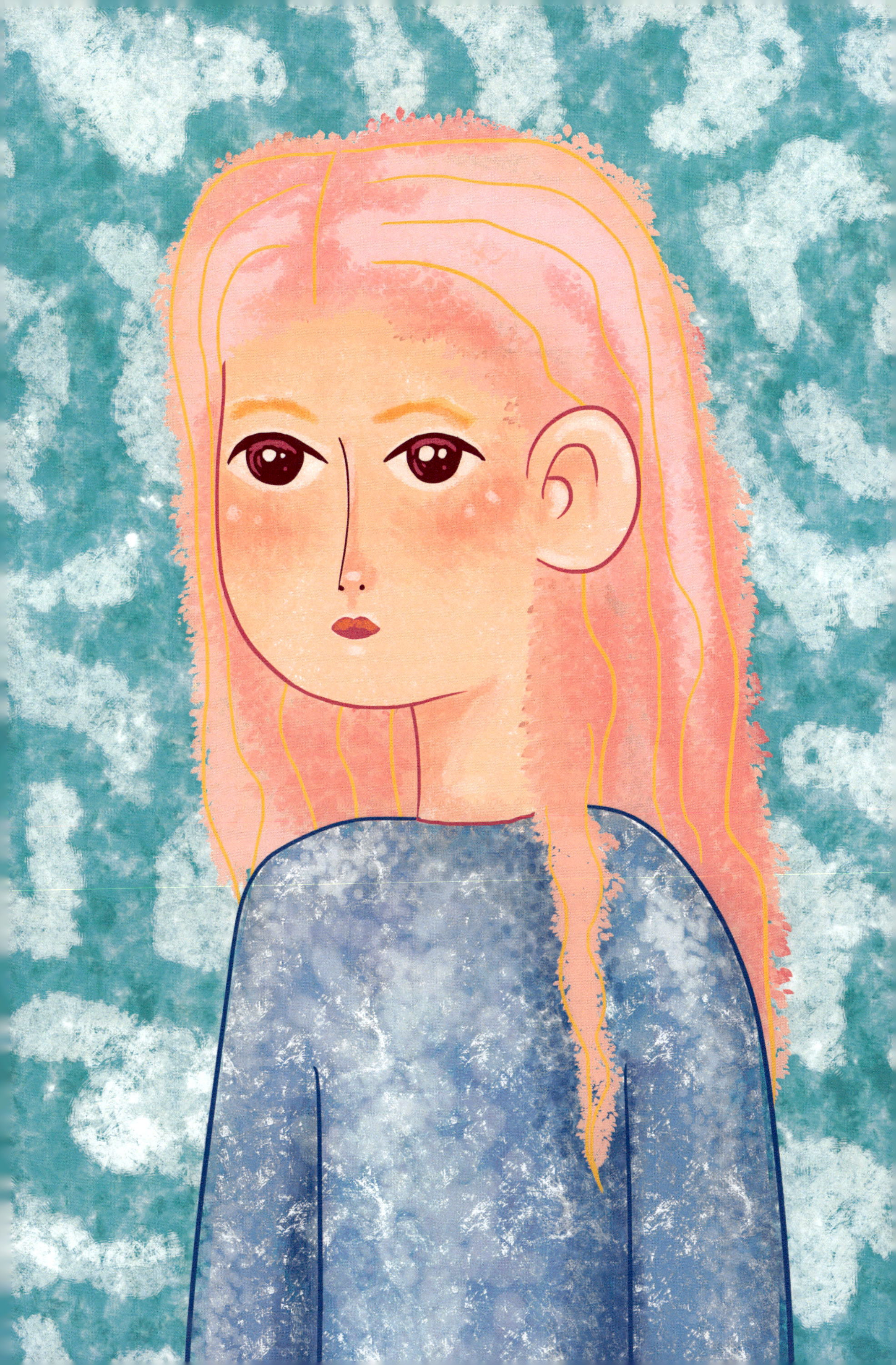

Zeruiah

Joab, Abishai, and Asahel were three mighty warriors from Israel. The Bible mentions them often because of their important roles alongside King David, one of Israel's most memorable kings. They joined David even before he was crowned, when he lived in hiding trying to save his life. Later, when David was appointed as the leader of Israel, he chose them as army officers, soldiers, and recognized commanders. Thanks to them, the king achieved much of his success.

But this story begins long before those battles. It begins with a mother taking care of her three little ones. Zeruiah was one of those strong and brave mothers who raise strong and brave children. Zeruiah often watched her little ones, Joab, Abishai, and Asahel, play battles and fight each other like true warriors. She looked at them fondly; she knew how important it was to be on the right side and fight for the right thing. Whenever she had an opportunity, she reminded them they always had to serve the people and have God in their hearts.

The brothers Joab, Abishai, and Asahel became determined men. They held positions of responsibility and contributed to the expansion of the kingdom of Israel. We don't know who their father was, even though in the Old Testament, in a world dominated by men, the father's name is usually included with the sons. But today, every time we read the name of one of these three brothers and everything they contributed to, the name that appears next to theirs is that of the woman who impacted their lives and will be remembered forever: Joab, Abishai, and Asahel, sons of Zeruiah.

1 Samuel 26:6,
2 Samuel 2:13,18; 3:39; 8:16; 14:1; 16:9, 10,
1 Kings 1:7; 2:5, 22,
1 Chronicles 2:16

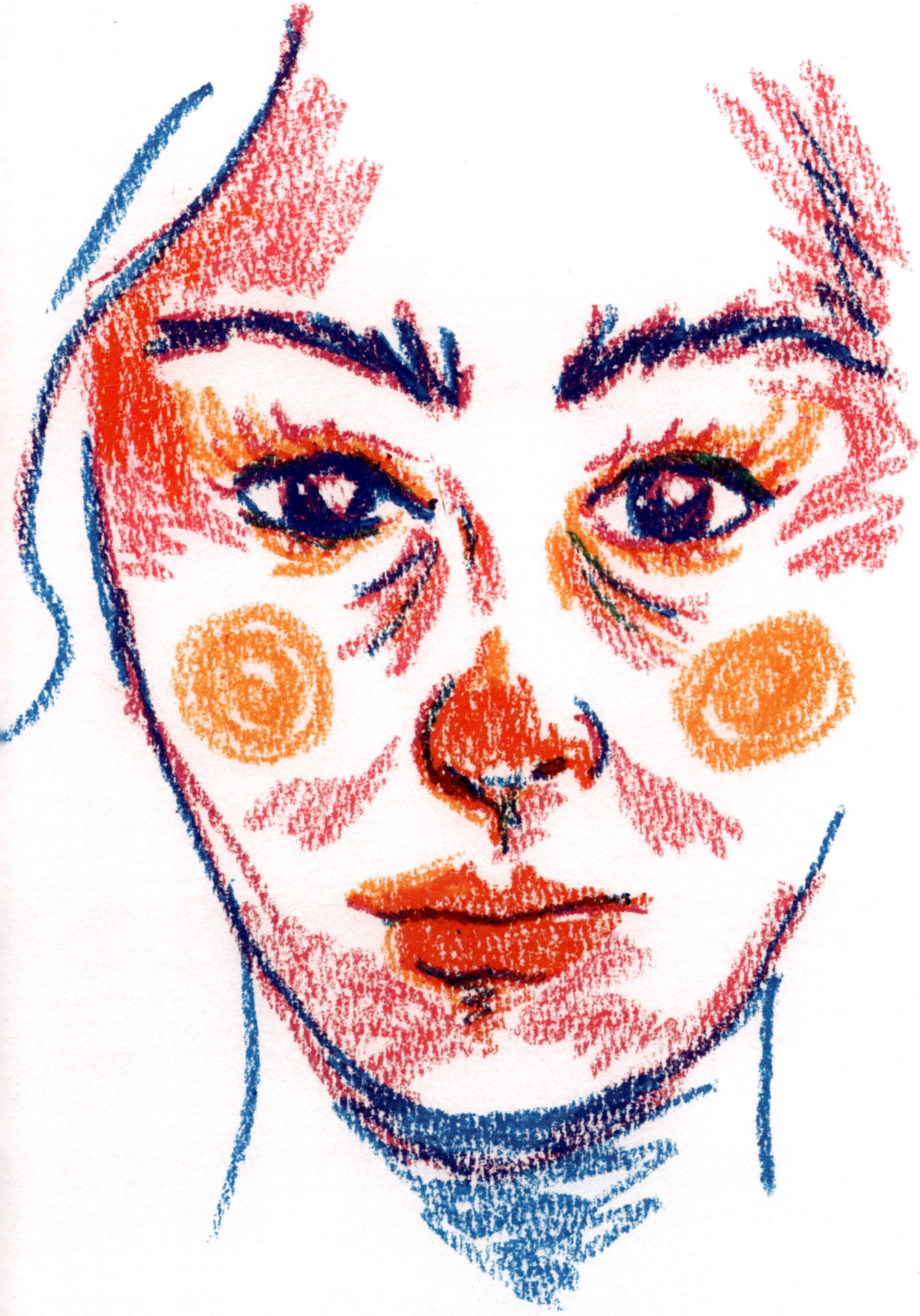

Abigail

Once upon a time in Maon, a town located in the mountains, there was a beautiful and intelligent woman married to an insolent man with bad intentions. Abigail, who stood out for both her inner and outer beauty, lived a comfortable life thanks to the great fortune of her rich husband. However, every day she suffered the consequences of his bad character, disgraceful habits, and lack of love toward those he constantly mistreated. Abigail knew very well how difficult life could be, even with a lot of money.

One day, Abigail had to secretly run away from home without Nabal, her husband, finding out in order to solve one of the many problems his bad attitude had caused. On this occasion, Nabal had horribly mistreated the future king of Israel, David, chosen and anointed by God to lead His people. When Abigail found out, she rushed to David to ask forgiveness for her husband's rude response and to stop the terrible consequences that would come. An army was headed toward her house at that very moment. Abigail acted with prudence and great wisdom in a decision as difficult as it was brave. She was able to recognize and act against the unjust limits her husband imposed, but she never stopped being a good wife and acknowledging Nabal, despite being the type of person and husband he had become.

A very short while later, Abigail became a widow and was finally free from such a difficult marriage. Abigail remarried, this time to David. Thus, after sharing some time with a man with a bad heart, she lived for many years married to David, whom we know today as a man after God's own heart. Although we know that Abigail's life was not perfect from then on, just as her marriage to David was not, God placed a man with a good heart by her side, a man who knew how to recognize the value of a wise, loyal, and humble woman like Abigail.

1 Samuel 25:2-42

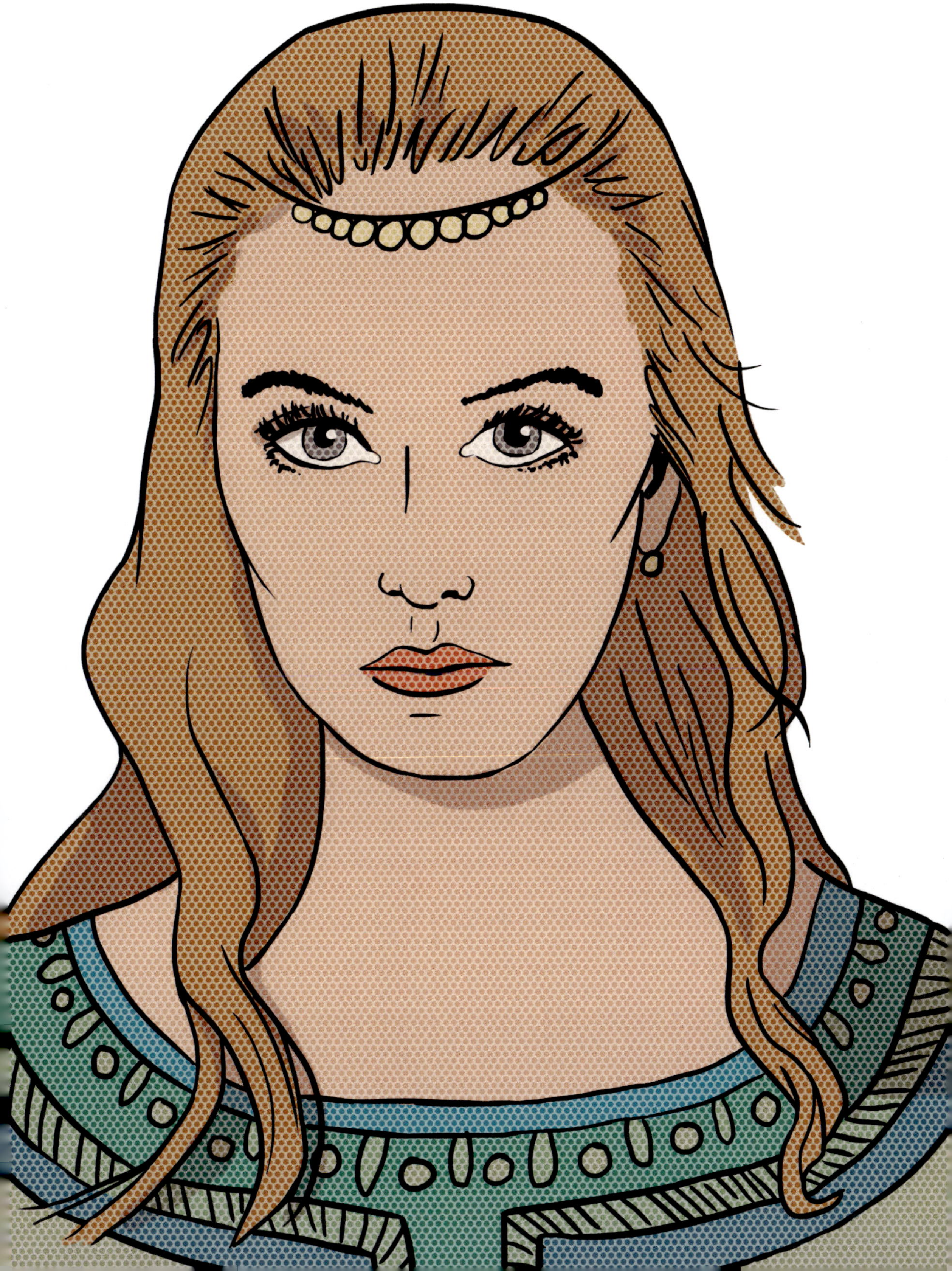

Bathsheba

Bathsheba felt completely confused. For years, death had been her greatest fear whenever her husband, Uriah, went to war. But this time, it was different. David, the king, had given orders for Uriah to be placed on the frontlines of the battle, where the most skilled soldiers went in groups to face the hardest part of combat. But Uriah had not had anyone with him. He had found himself alone, also by order of the king, and had died abandoned by his companions, betrayed by a king to whom he had always been faithful.

Bathsheba blamed herself for it. King David wanted her for himself, but she was already married. It had all happened so suddenly that Bathsheba could hardly believe it. She felt like a puppet being used by a powerful man. Wasn't David a good king? Didn't he love God above all things? Why, then, did he act this way? Like a rich man stealing his poor neighbor's only sheep to feed his guests, that is how David was behaving. Many times, even people who love God make mistakes that hurt others around them.

Bathsheba felt lost. She was very scared. How she wanted to go back in time. She wished she had hidden and David had never seen her, never known she existed. But now it was too late.

God saw inside her. Inside her and inside David. The pain of sin is unavoidable, but God can restore the heart. God saw Bathsheba's tears. He saw David's heart completely repentant of his terrible choices. God offered His forgiveness and allowed them to move on. David married Bathsheba. After some time, they had a baby; they called him Solomon. God loved Solomon and, through him, made Bathsheba the mother of a very wise king who reigned for many years in Israel. Furthermore, later on, an even greater King would be born from her offspring: Christ, the King of kings.

2 Samuel 11:1-12:25

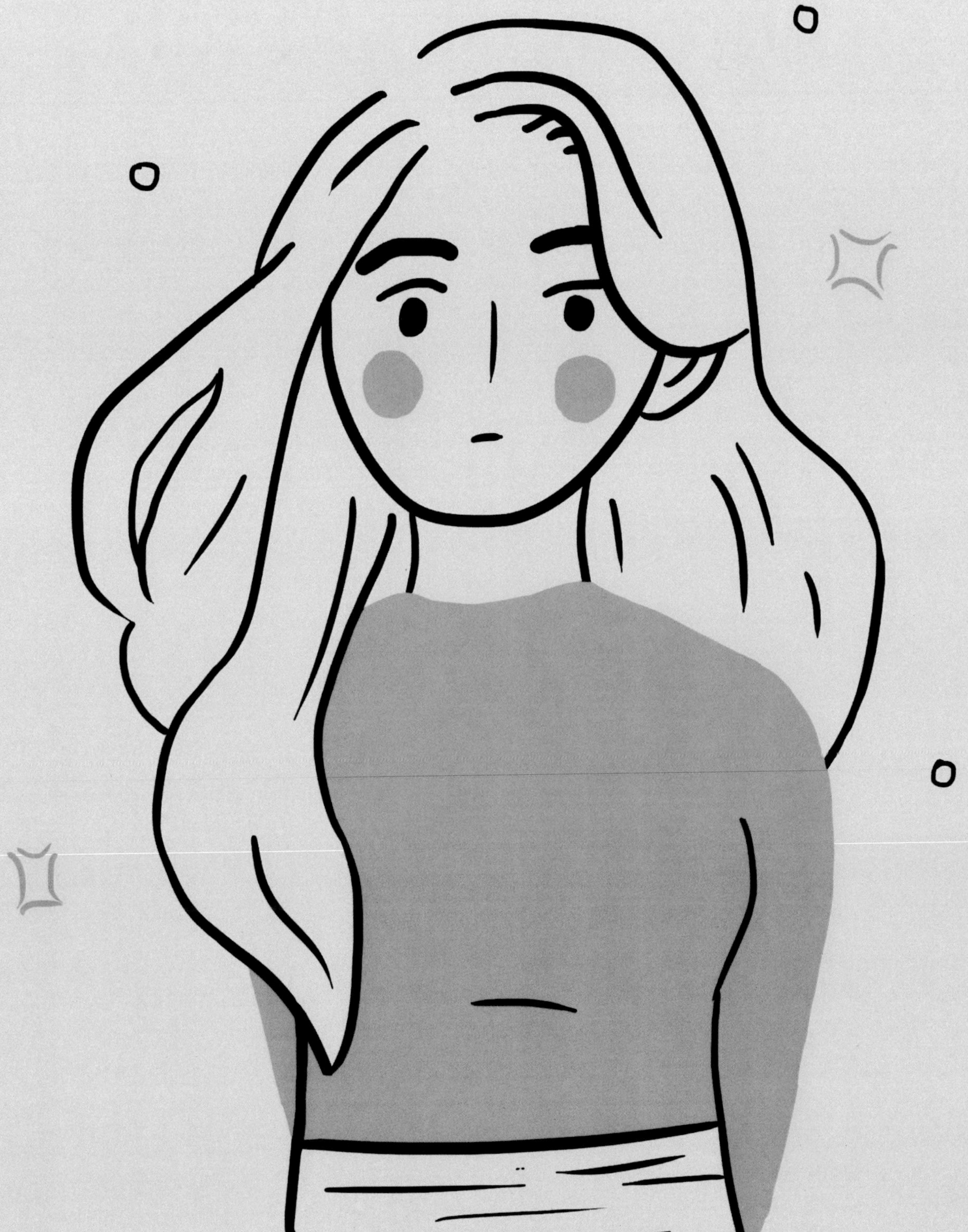

Tamar of Judah

There are people who lie, people who cheat, people who take advantage of others, people who steal and take what isn't theirs. There are people capable of ruining someone's life just for their own pleasure. Some people hurt in ways that are hard to understand, hard to deal with, hard to explain. This is how Amnon hurt his sister Tamar. There were no words to describe how terribly her heart ached. And even if there were, no one could understand them. That day left a permanent mark on Tamar's life. A little piece of herself was gone forever.

Tamar was one of the daughters of David, from the tribe of Judah. As the daughter of a king, her entire life had been about preparing for a good marriage. She had inherited her beauty from her father, and throughout her life, she had developed a deep sense of humility and integrity. The first years of her youth had barely blossomed when a black shadow fell over her. All her plans and dreams disappeared that day.

She changed her cheerful and colorful clothes to black dresses. She felt embarrassed, scared, and sad. Nothing could give her joy or rest. She felt so alone. No one else could understand her. Her brother, whom she was willing to forgive, wanted nothing to do with her. Her father, the great King David, whom everyone acclaimed, did nothing either. Finally, Absalom, her older brother, took her into his home, though he didn't quite understand how she felt either.

Tamar was condemned to live a life of sadness, loneliness, and rejection. A life she didn't deserve and one that she had to suffer unfairly because of someone who hadn't thought of her. Tamar felt miserable. She felt alone and misunderstood. But God understood her. He stayed by her side and suffered with each of her tears. God caused her story to be written down and remembered, to be shared with so many other women who, like Tamar, felt that someone else had taken their lives unfairly. To raise their voices and keep their tears from being wasted.

2 Samuel 13:1-22

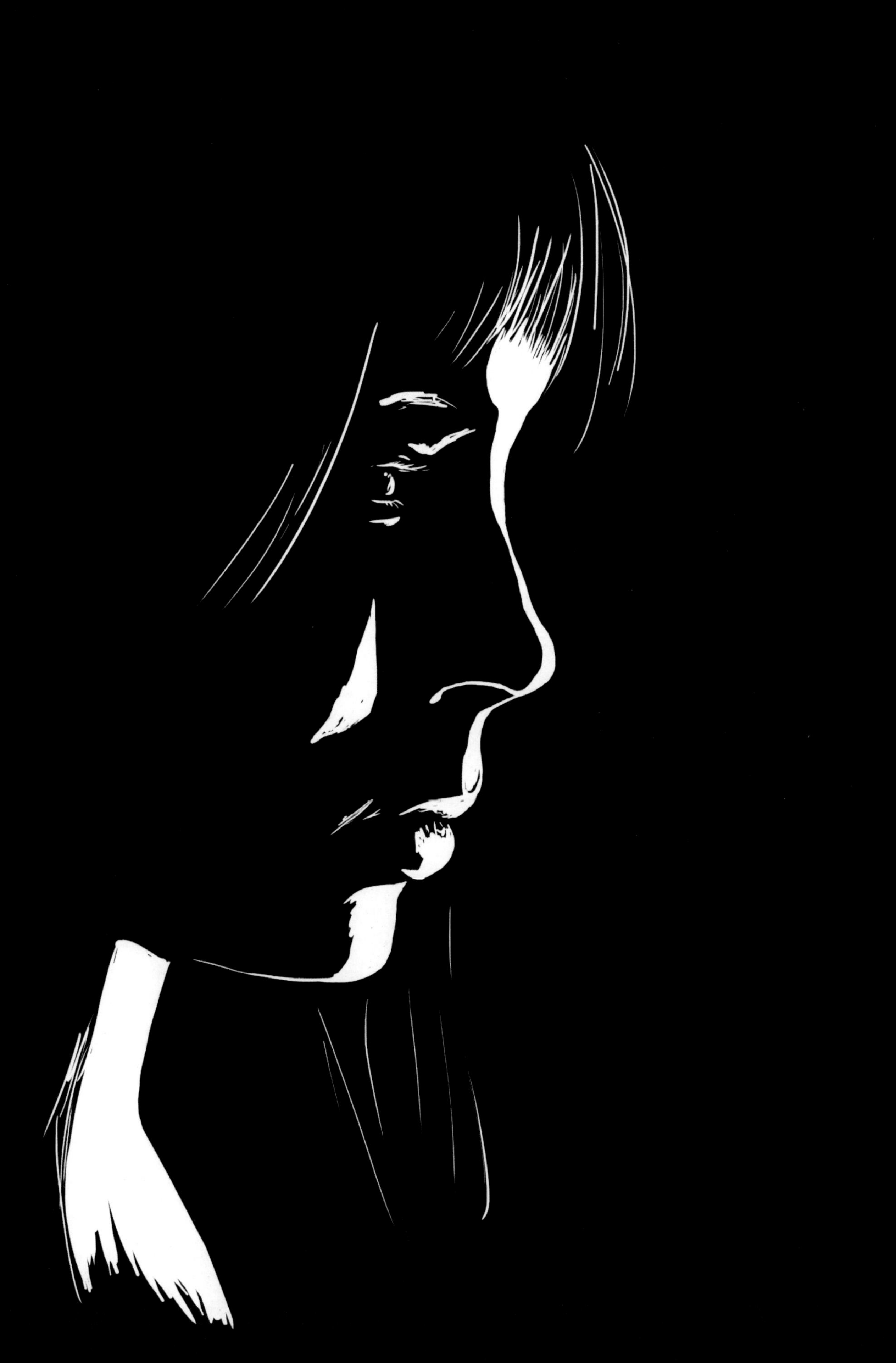

Rizpah

Rizpah was the second wife of Israel's first king, Saul. Together they had two sons: Armoni and Mephibosheth. Saul had turned out to be not such a good king; he had made some wrong decisions during his reign, and for that, Israel was suffering the consequences. But Saul was already dead, and now David ruled over Israel. Surely David should have consulted God about what to do, but instead, he followed the ideas of a group of Gibeonites, a neighboring nation that didn't know God. They thought it would be a good idea to humiliate Saul's memory by punishing all his sons. David agreed and put the plan into action. The death of these men would bring peace to Israel.

On the same day, Rizpah saw both of her sons killed. Rizpah cried and screamed inconsolably. But as if that weren't enough, to further embarrass and humiliate Saul, David ordered their dead bodies to be dumped on the mountain. As a mother, Rizpah's heart was broken. Her poor children. How was this possible? They were not to blame for their father's bad decisions. Was there no other way to bring peace to Israel?

Rizpah spread a cloth used to express repentance on the ground. For months she cried and stood by the lifeless bodies of her children. Day and night, she frightened away the birds and wild animals that approached. Under the strong summer sun, despite the terrible heat and exhaustion, she waved her arms, kicked, and screamed whenever she saw something approaching.

Someone came to King David and told him about Rizpah. Hearing about this mother's pain, David finally understood that revenge only brings more pain. Long ago, God had said that children cannot pay for their parents' mistakes. David immediately ordered that the bodies of Saul's sons be picked up and buried. God used Rizpah to make His people understand that repentance is the only thing that really changes situations. God listened to His people and finally brought peace to His nation. Rizpah's heart rested as well.

2 Samuel 21:8-14

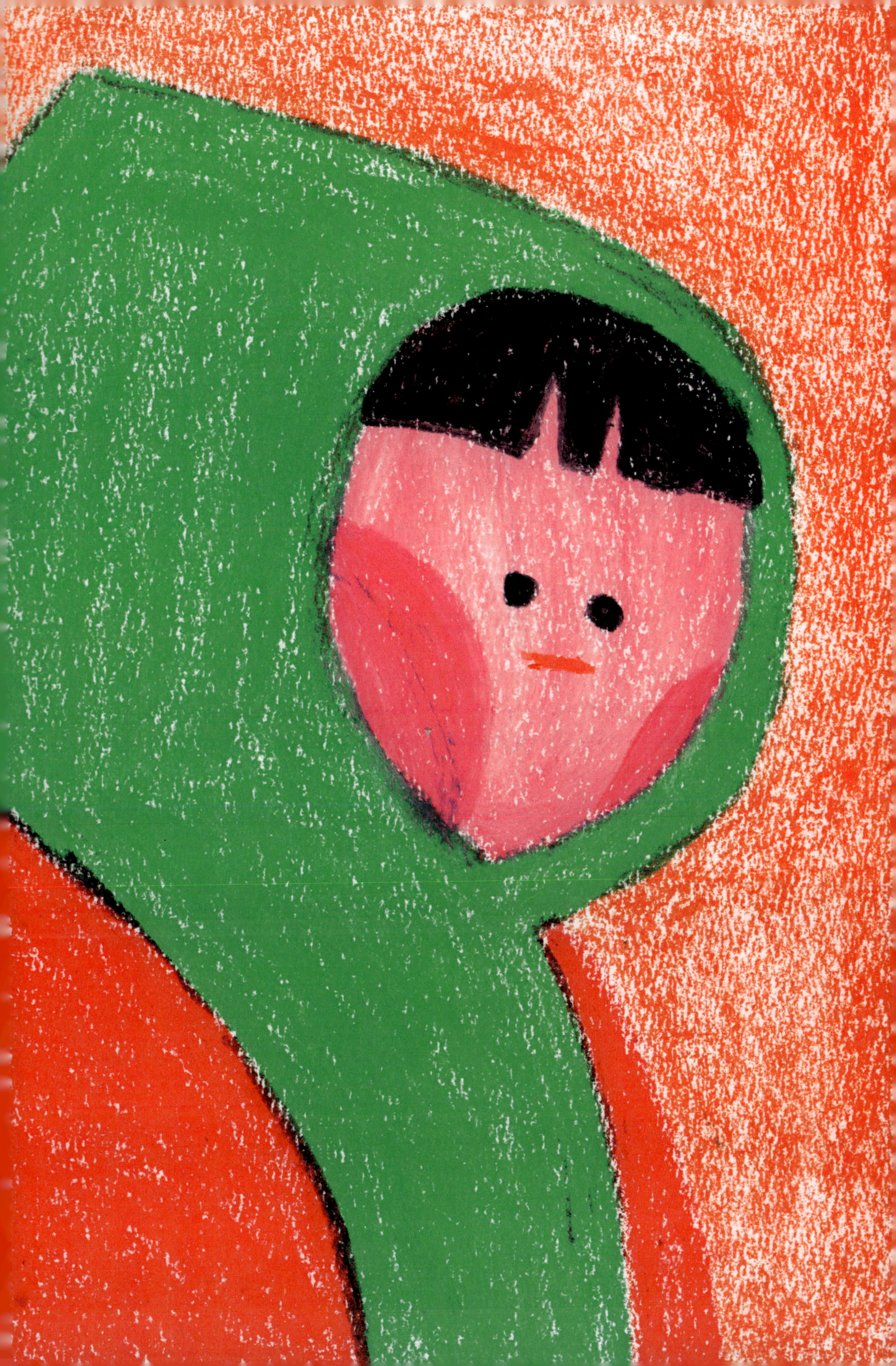

Jehosheba

She cradled the baby in her arms, trembling and wondering what to do. Jehosheba waited impatiently in her room for her husband to arrive to tell him what she had just done. She had stolen little Joash and had him hidden there with her. The baby played with the blanket he was wrapped in, too young to understand that, just a few minutes before, Jehosheba had saved his life.

The king of Judah had just died, and the whole nation was agitated. Jehosheba was not proud of the reign of her brother Ahaziah, who had not followed God and was leading the people in disobedience and self-destruction. But the worst was yet to come. Athaliah, her proud and tyrannical stepmother, had decided to become the new queen. She believed she would reign better than any of her grandsons, the legitimate heirs to the throne. Without thinking twice, she devised a plan to get rid of them so no one would be in the way.

When Jehoiada, the high priest, arrived home, he found his wife trembling with the child in her arms, thinking of what to do next. Perhaps the safest thing would be to hide the baby in the temple of God. Athaliah didn't worship God, so the chances of her going near the temple were really small. And so they did.

Athaliah got what she wanted and became queen. For years she ruled over Judah, doing whatever she pleased. She was a lousy leader and a very bad example for the people of God. But she didn't realize that the true successor to the throne was growing up happy and healthy within the temple walls. Jehosheba and Jehoiada made sure that he lacked nothing: they were the only family Joash knew, and they taught him to be a good, God-fearing man and a good king.

When Joash was seven years old, the proclamation of the new king — the legitimate king, the successor to the crown, the only survivor of the line of David — was announced throughout the nation. Joash reigned, serving and pleasing God. The people followed his good example and turned to God. All this is because a brave woman risked her life to save and raise the one who should be king.

2 Kings 11:1-20,
2 Chronicles 22:10-23:11

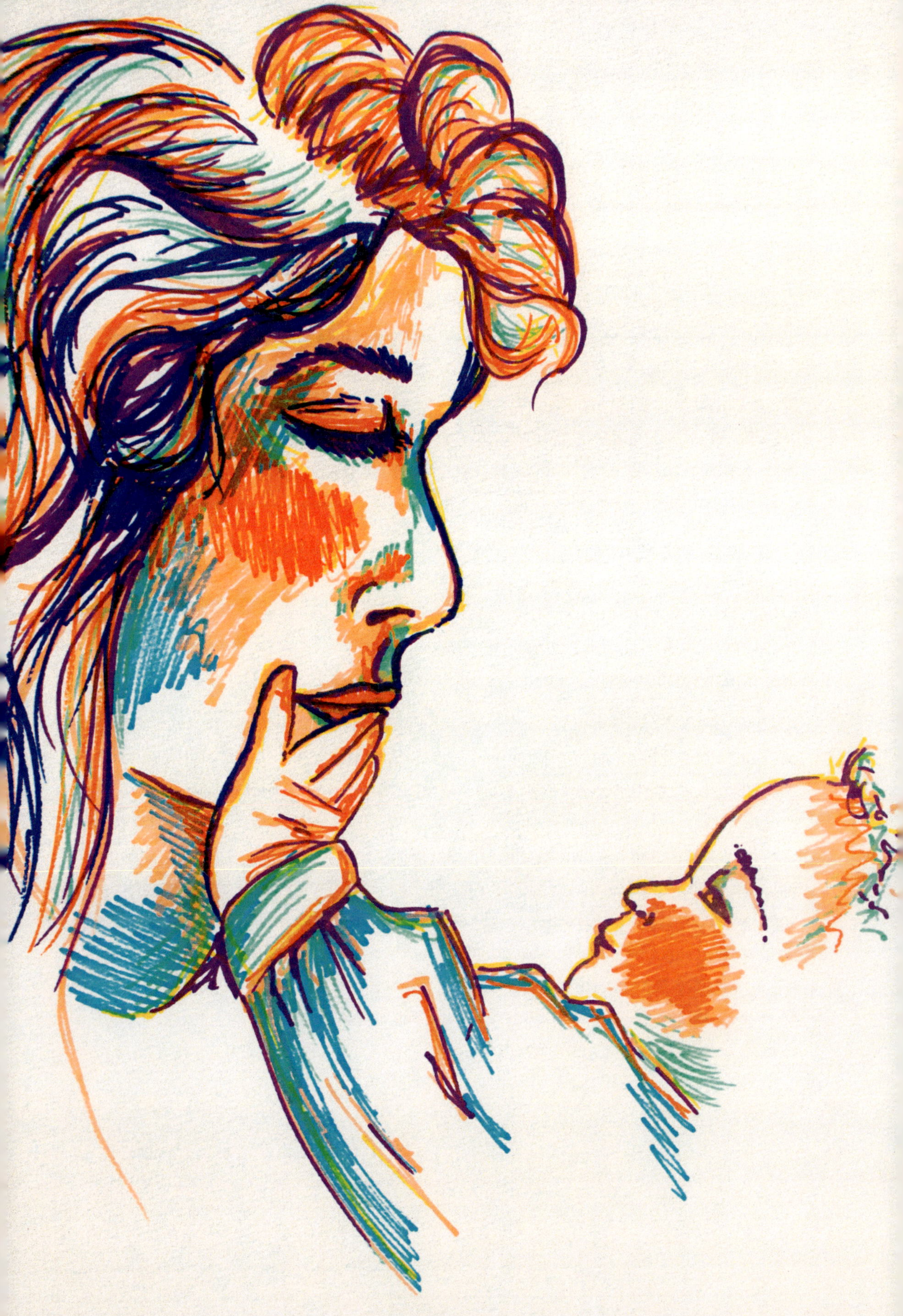

Azubah

For many years, the nation of Israel was led by kings. Even though God had wanted to be the His people's only guide, the Israelites asked for a king like the rest of the nations had. Thus, kings succeeded each other for years. Some kings followed God, and then all the people obeyed His commandments, and the nation prospered. But the truth is that most of the kings behaved in selfish and authoritarian ways; they built altars for the people to worship other gods and brought destruction upon Israel. This is how Israel was divided into two opposing nations: Israel and Judah, each with their own kings. Some followed God, but most of them forgot about Him.

Next to each king, in the shadow, lived his wife. These women closely observed the behavior of their husbands, the way they governed the nation, and the consequences that these actions brought on the people. There was very little a king's wife could do in those days, but they knew that one day their own sons would be the nation's leaders. The way these women prepared these future kings could have a great impact on an entire nation.

Azubah was one of these women. She had the opportunity to witness firsthand how the poor decisions of her husband, King Asa, negatively affected all of Judah. Although at first Asa's reign had started on the right track, he rejected the words God sent him through the prophet Hanani, putting him in prison. Azubah saw how this caused great suffering not only for her husband but also for the entire nation. Azubah was one of a group of women who knew how to raise their children not to follow the bad example of other kings. Her son, Jehoshaphat, showed respect and love for God during his reign, a reflection of what Azubah had taught him; as did Jehoaddan, the mother of king Amaziah; Jecoliah, the mother of king Uzziah; Jerusha, the mother of king Jotham; and Hephzibah, the mother of king Manasseh. Women God placed in a privileged place and who, unlike many others, knew how to positively influence an entire nation.

1 Kings 22:42,
2 Chronicles 20:31

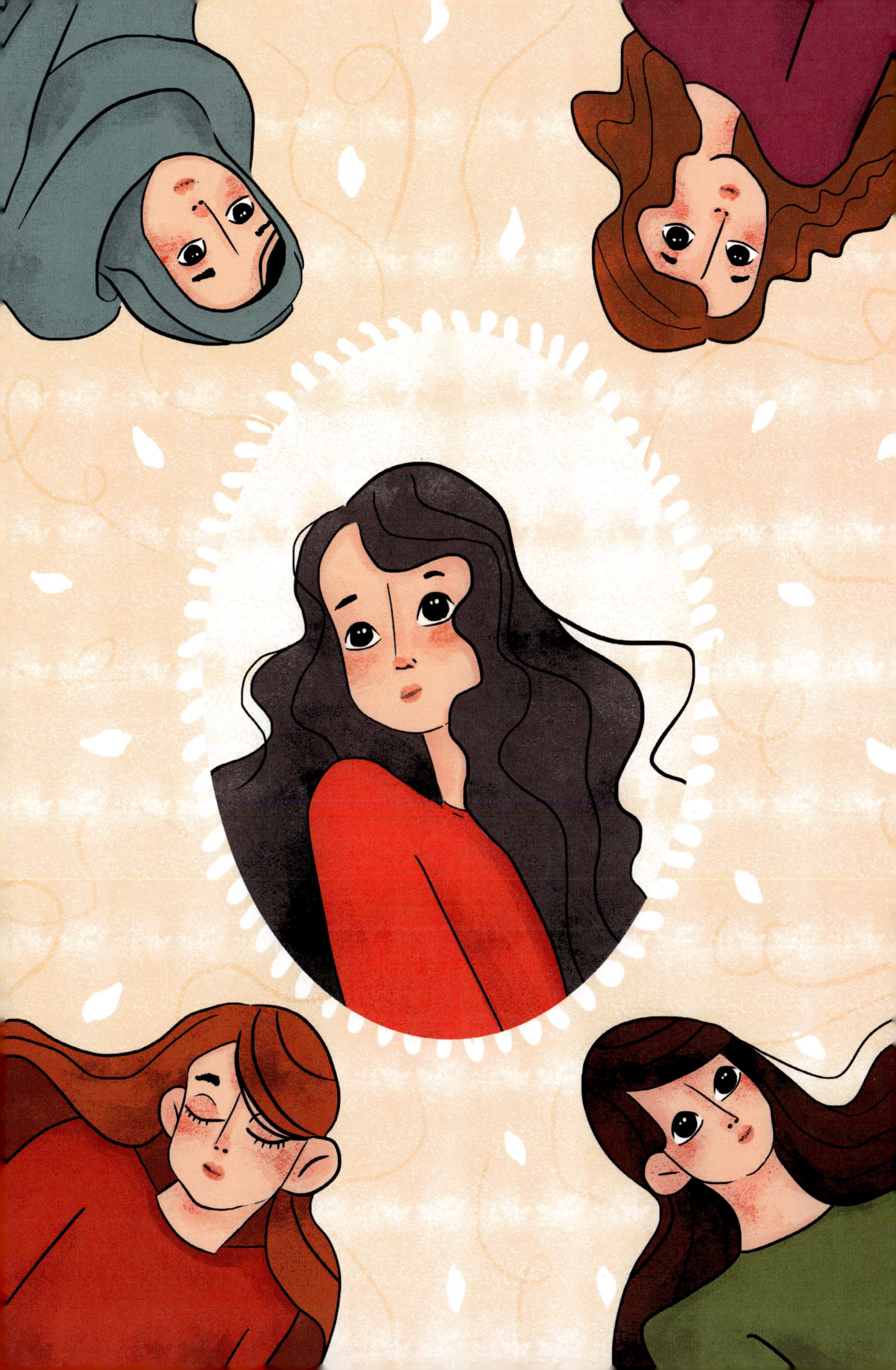

Abijah

Little Abi was born into an important family of priests in Israel; she remembered hundreds of stories that she had heard from her relatives about how God cares for His own, stories. Her father, Zechariah, didn't stop telling everyone that God always cared for and protected His people, and they should trust only Him. Zechariah and his wife wanted these words to permeate Abijah's life and gave her a name with a special meaning: "My Father is the Lord."

As Abi grew older and married, she realized that not everyone lives in a way that pleases God. Her husband, Ahaz, was the king of Judah, but he wasn't a good king, and his heart was far from God. Many people died because of Ahaz, but the worst thing was that he made the whole nation turn away from God, worship idols, and do terrible things. Abijah watched and remembered everything her father had taught her.

When her son was born, Abijah knew he would become king one day. Abijah dreamed that her son would be a good leader. She named him Hezekiah, which means "My strength is in God." Perhaps then, Hezekiah would always remember whom to turn to and whom to trust throughout the years of his reign.

Years passed, and Hezekiah finally became king. Abijah watched him to reign and was glad to see what a good king he was. Hezekiah trusted God, and God cared for him in a special way. Abijah witnessed how Hezekiah repaired the temple, where the tribe of Judah returned to worship God, and how he removed the many idols that his father and other previous kings had introduced. Hezekiah didn't follow the bad example of others and became the best of the kings of Judah; there was no one like him, either before or after his reign. Abijah had chosen a good name for him.

2 Kings 18:2,
2 Chronicles 29:1

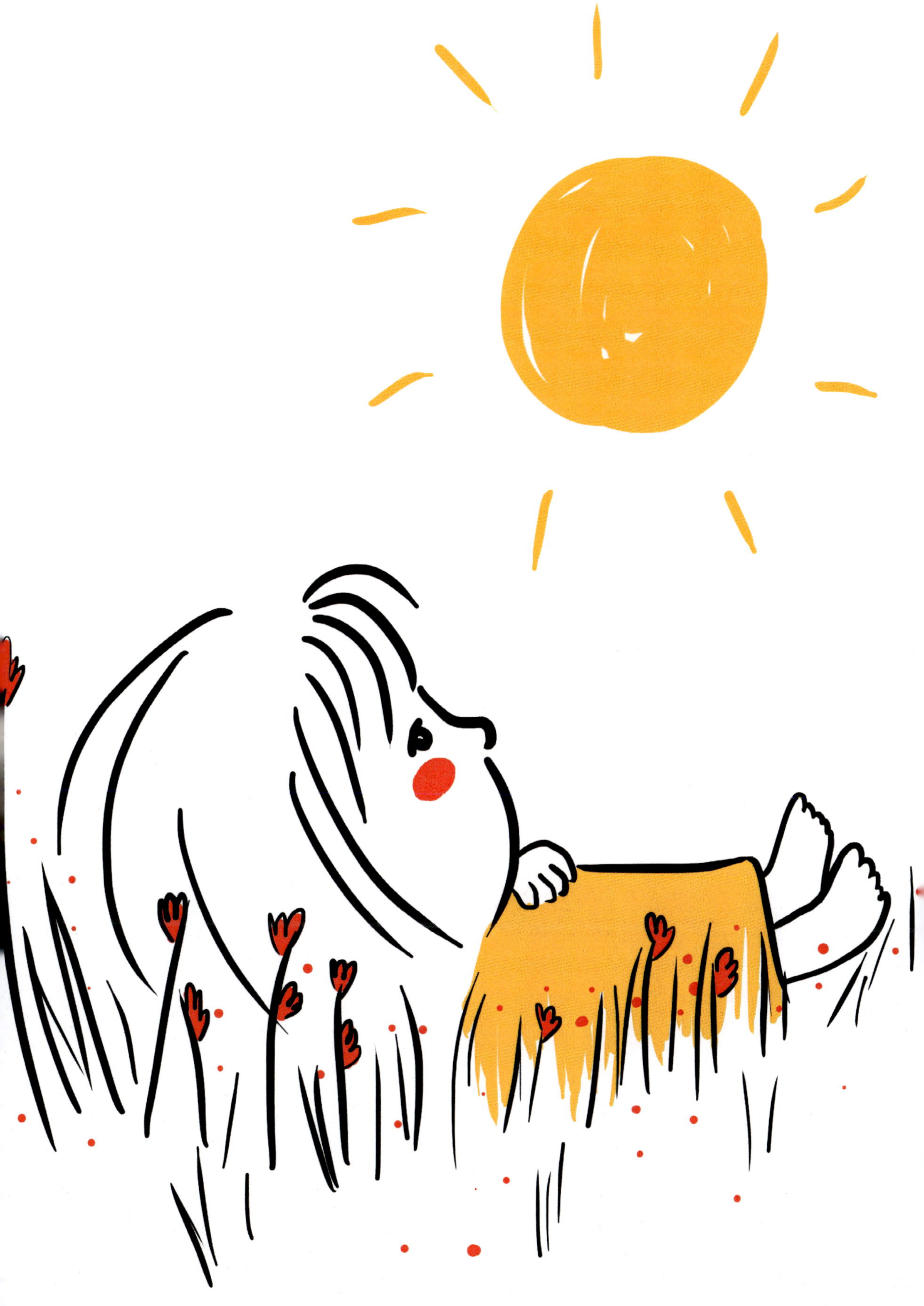

Jedidah

Jedidah lived with her husband, King Amon. Amon was a proud and smug king, like his father. Life at the palace was unbearable; for Jedidah, every day was a real torment. Amon did not follow God and incited the people to worship idols; in addition, his provocative attitude made his workers hate him. No one wanted to be near him. Barely two years had passed since the beginning of Amon's reign, but the situation was awful. When Jedidah and Amon's son was born, Jedidah named him Josiah, which means "may the Lord heal," perhaps hoping that her little boy would one day become a good king and rid the nation of Judah of the atrocities in which it was immersed. Every day, Jedidah cared for and protected little Josiah, trying to teach him something very important for the good of the nation: obedience to God.

No one expected what happened next. On what seemed like an ordinary day, an argument at the palace suddenly ended in tragedy. The ministers who worked alongside the king revolted against him and ended his life. Jedidah was a widow instantly, Josiah lost his father, and the nation of Judah was left without a king. The people mobilized immediately, and soon after, the king's son, little Josiah, only eight years old, was named king of Judah.

Jedidah knew how difficult it was for a boy to be king, but she was sure that, with God's help, anyone could rule better than her own husband had. Jedidah had to exert herself as a mother during the following years as her son had to suddenly assume such an important responsibility. And so it was. Josiah grew in stature, but his love and obedience to God also grew in him, as well as his care and help for the Israelites. Josiah was a good king. He eliminated the bad habits his father and grandfather established and didn't follow their terrible example. Instead, he honored the name his mother had chosen for him and let God heal His people of sin.

2 Kings 22:1-2

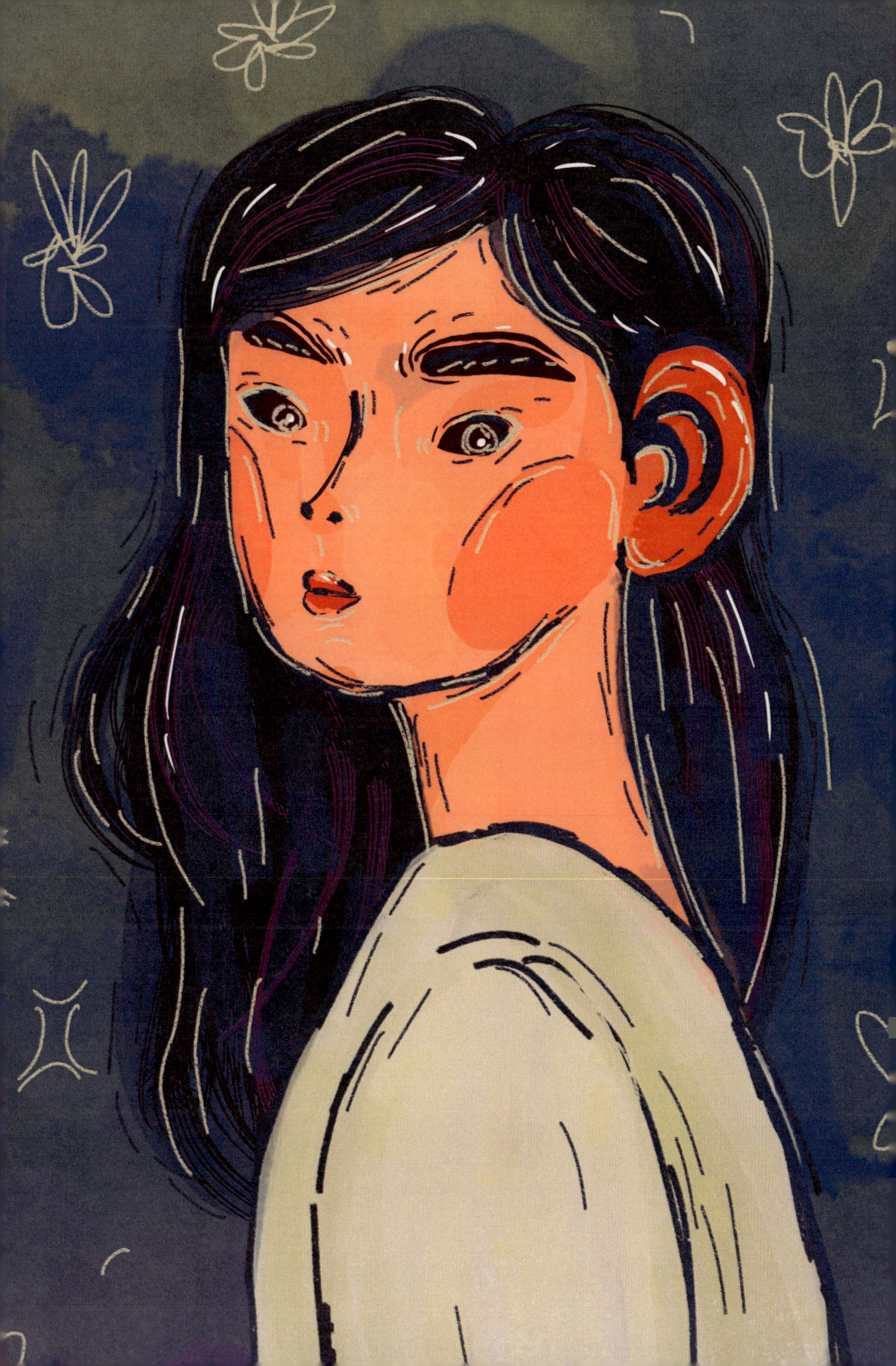

Huldah

The high priest came running to Huldah's house. Huldah lived in Jerusalem. These were very difficult times for her as a prophetess; no one was willing to listen to God. But that day seemed different from all the others. King Josiah had just found a document in the temple. It was a very old document that nobody remembered: the scroll of the Scriptures, the Word of God. Josiah was very worried. Huldah perfectly understood why. The people had forgotten their Lord. For the past few years, Judah had been ruled by a series of kings who had encouraged horrible practices and the worship of false gods.

Huldah took a deep breath. God was not happy with them, and King Josiah must know. But it wasn't easy for a king to listen to what Huldah had to say. Many kings before had killed other prophets precisely for saying what Huldah had to say to Josiah. But God had entrusted His Word to her, and she could not keep silent. Huldah loved her nation, but its situation hurt her deeply; with tears in her eyes, she uttered some words that caused her as much pain as they did to Josiah:

"This is what God says: 'You have abandoned me. You walked away from me, and that's why terrible things are about to happen to you. Your injustice, selfishness, and lack of love for God have led you to this.'"

There, she said it. Huldah closed her eyes and took another breath. Her voice was steady, but she trembled on the inside. Then, God spoke to her again, and she added:

"But tell Josiah that God knows how worried he is and has seen his repentance and humility. That's why He's not going to punish us now."

When Josiah received Huldah's words, a nationwide reformation began. He called an emergency meeting at the temple. There, he read the Word of God aloud so everyone could hear it. He promised that he would follow God and obey Him from then on. He asked that everyone else commit as well. Huldah breathed again: a new phase was beginning in Jerusalem.

2 Kings 22:8-23:3,
2 Chronicles 34:14-33

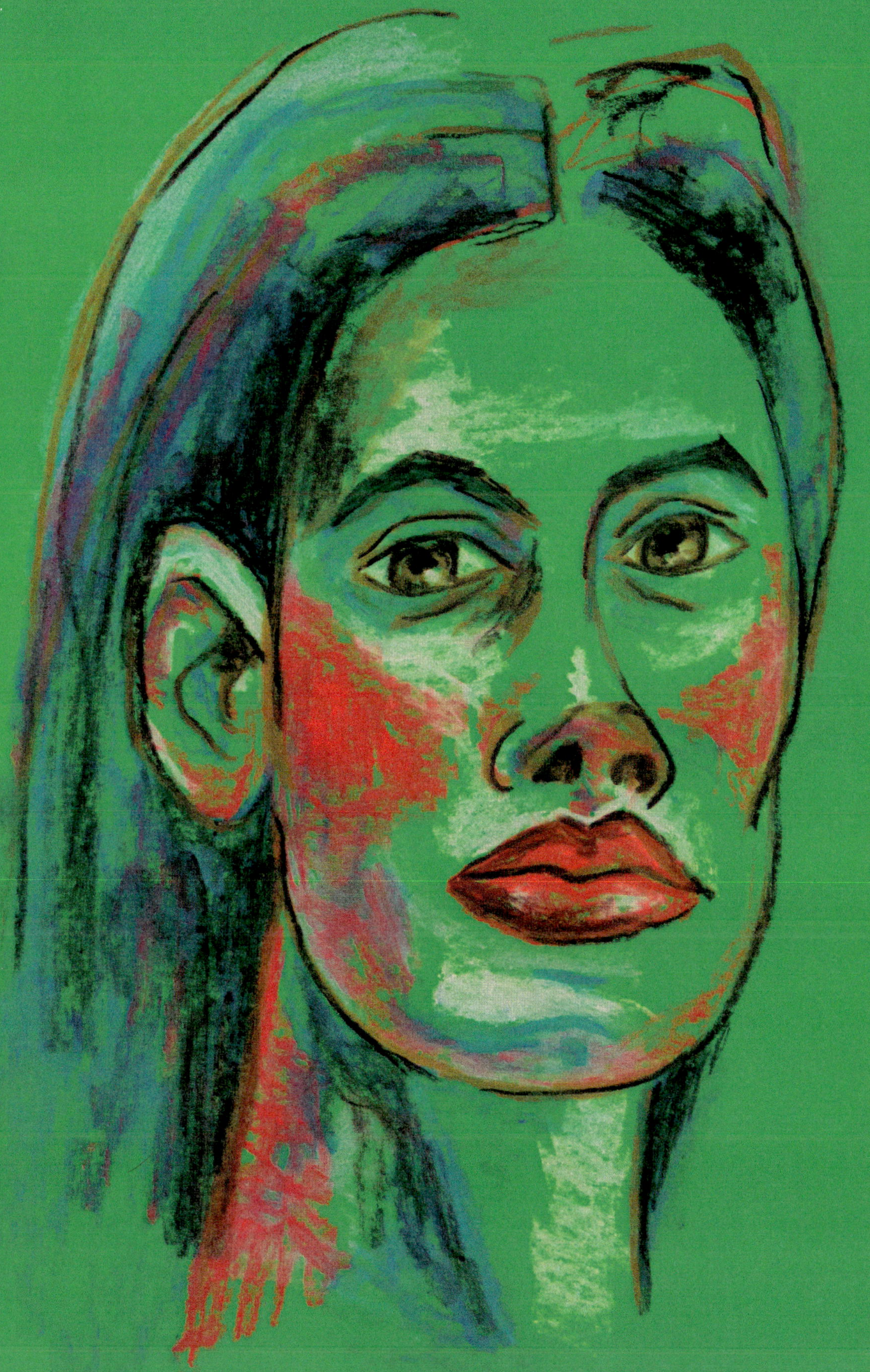

Bithiah

"Pharaoh's daughter." That had been her identity for years. Everyone in Egypt knew and respected her. Not because of anything she had done or achieved but because she was born into a certain family, the family of the governor of her nation. All eyes were on her. Attention, regard, bows, whatever was needed to recognize her greatness. Everyone wanted to please her, and their treatment of her was exceptional. Power and wealth were evident in every corner of the palace, where she had always lived. But in return, she had to pay the price. She had to live up to her social position. For her father, it was much simpler. For him, being the pharaoh of Egypt was an honor and his highest aspiration. He was completely convinced that theirs was a superior nation and that his empire shone above others. But none of that mattered to her. And that's why she changed her name.

"Daughter of the Lord." That's what her new name Bithiah, meant. Bithiah married Mered, an Israelite from the tribe of Judah. At first, she felt like a foreigner. But little by little, she learned to live among them as one of them. And that is what she was now: one more among the Israelites. Now she was part of God's people. The Israelites could feel privileged. God had chosen them from among all the nations of the earth to take care of them in a special way and offer them something that no other nation had: the possibility of a relationship with Him and the privilege of being a blessing to others. For years, God had protected them and been present, even physically, at all times. What a great honor. That was the nation to which Bithiah wanted to belong. That was the God she wanted to have. She no longer wanted to be known as the daughter of Pharaoh but as the daughter of someone much greater, someone even more powerful. Now she had a new identity. And this was one that she herself had chosen and wanted to keep. That is why everyone now knew her as Bithiah, daughter of the Lord.

1 Chronicles 4:18

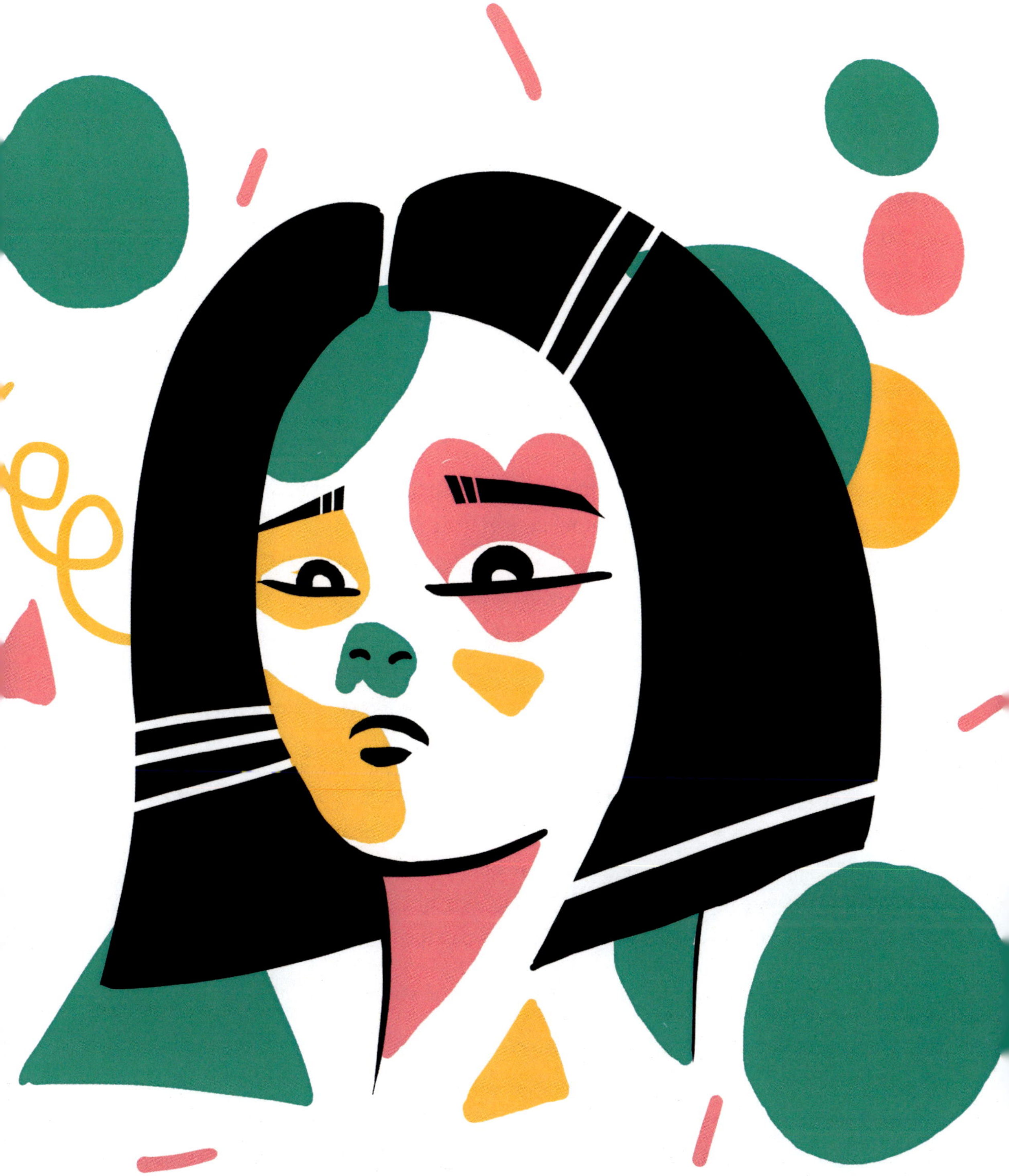

Hadassah

Hadassah's parents died when she was little, so a close relative adopted her. Although they were Jews, they didn't live in a Jewish region but in Susa, a city that belonged to the Persian empire, where the Jews had been taken captive some years before. But the Persians didn't know God, and many of them didn't like the Jews either.

The king of Persia was named Ahasuerus. He was a selfish and proud king. One day, Ahasuerus gathered the most beautiful girls in his nation because he wanted to choose one to marry. The chosen one would be the queen of Persia!

So, his workers went throughout the region, selecting some young women to take to the palace of King Ahasuerus. Among them was Hadassah. She was beautiful, intelligent, very nice and kind — that's why they took her too. But Hadassah knew that King Ahasuerus didn't like Jews, so she followed the advice of a relative and didn't tell anyone that she was one of them. Finally, King Ahasuerus chose Hadassah and named her Esther. That was how she became the queen of Persia. Now Hadassah had everything. They gave her the most valuable jewels, she had beautiful dresses, she used expensive perfumes, and she ate the most sophisticated foods.

Three years later, Ahasuerus did something terrible: he signed a law that all Jews must be killed. Hadassah was very scared when she found out. She didn't know what to do. The easiest thing would be to do nothing. After all, she was the queen. She had everything she wanted, and the king didn't know she was a Jew, so she was safe. But what if God had placed her in that position to save His people? What if it was no coincidence that she was the queen?

"I'll go talk to the king, and if I have to die, I'll die!" she said determinedly.

And so, she did. Hadassah appeared before the king, knowing that it was not allowed and that her life was in danger. She explained that she was Jewish and asked him not to kill her people. The king listened to her and saw something very special in her. He saw humility and courage. Her words shocked Ahasuerus' heart.

Thanks to Hadassah, many Jews were saved. And not only that, but many Persians also came to know God and became Jews.

Esther 2-9

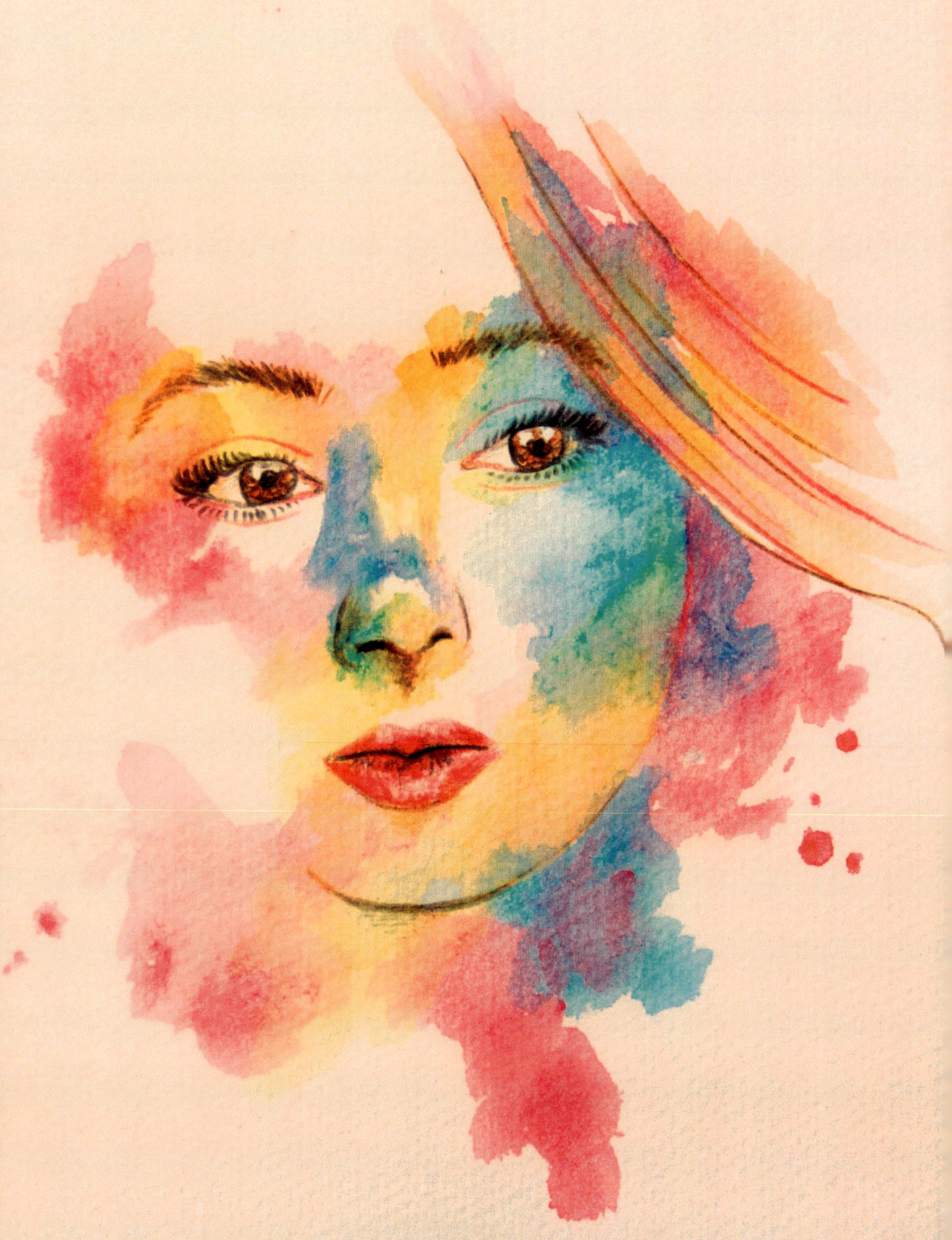

Jemimah, Keziah, and Keren Happuch

One day, God will gather those who follow Him to live a life without sadness or pain forever. But until then, life in this world can be hard at times. Jemimah, Keziah, and Keren Happuch knew this very well. Their family had gone through very difficult times shortly before they were born. All their siblings had died in a terrible accident, thieves had taken a good part of the family's possessions, and the rest had been totally consumed by a great fire. Shortly after that, Job, their father, had fallen very ill.

When Jemimah, Keziah, and Keren Happuch were born, God was restoring a new life for their family. Job, who, despite having lost everything, had stood firm and had strengthened his faith even more, accepted the girls as a gift after a time that seemed to take everything from him. Jemimah represented the peace that God had restored in the lives of Job and his family. Keziah, whose name came from cinnamon, represented the fragrance, a pleasant aroma that makes us think of hope and the possibility of joy despite pain. Keren Happuch represented the beauty of life with God. The three sisters were a daily reminder to Job and his family that despite life's difficulties, God remains faithful to us and controls everything around us. If we stand firm, God will reward our steadfastness and bring peace, delight, and beauty into our lives.

Jemimah, Keziah, and Keren Happuch were God's instruments to comfort and reward the faithful and constant heart of their father, Job. Their lives are a reminder to us of God's goodness and faithfulness. Job loved them in a special way, and at the end of his days, when he divided his extensive inheritance among his children, he gave his daughters an equal share to what he gave his sons, something that was strange in a time when women were not considered heirs.

Job 42:13-15

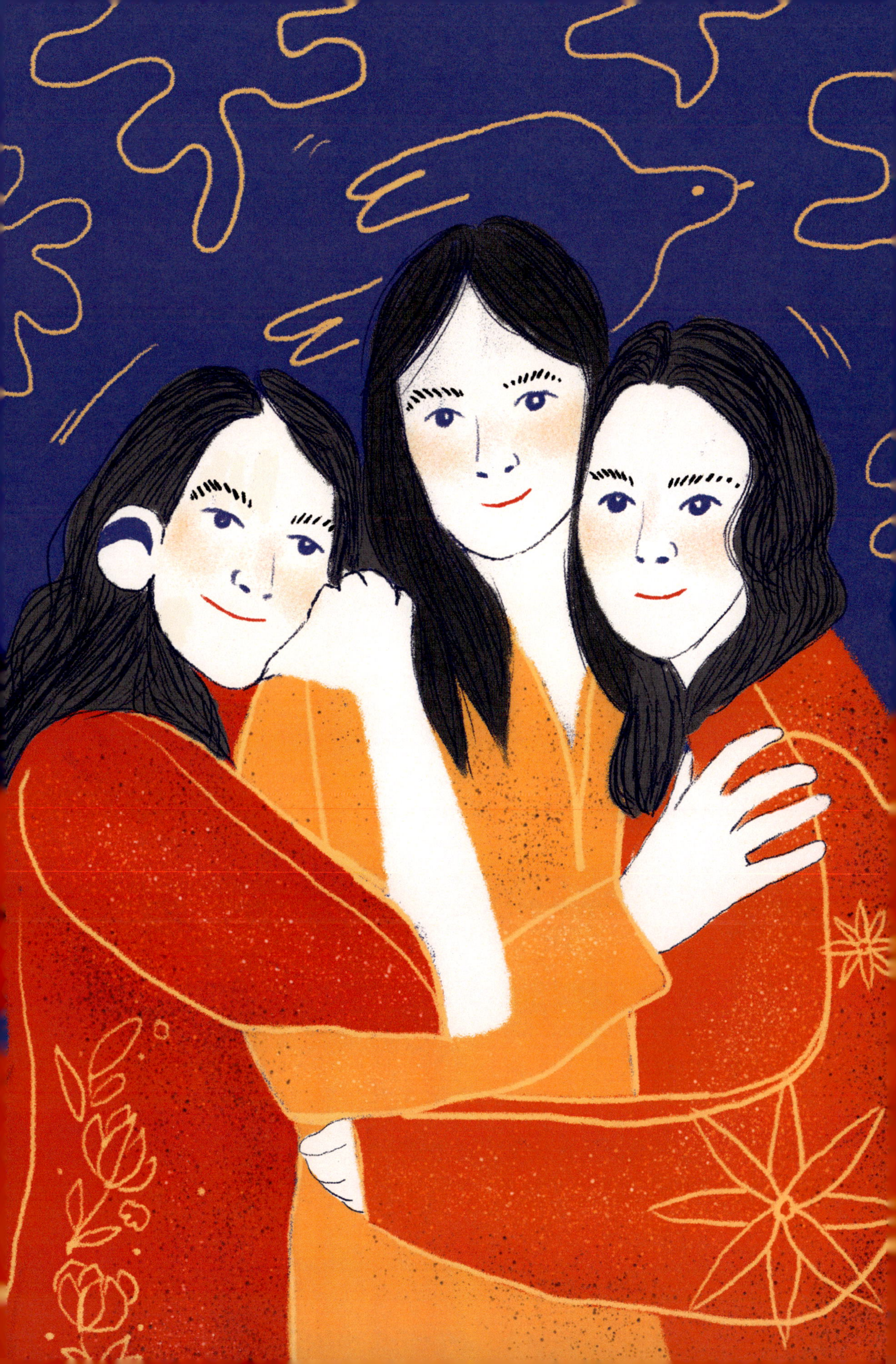

Mary

Mary was totally confused. What kind of greeting was that? Her legs barely responded as they held her upright before the visitor. Who was he? Or rather, what was it? Someone sent from God. Sent for what? Thousands of thoughts flitted through her mind as her visitor continued to speak.

"Don't be afraid," he said. "The Lord has noticed you."

Mary felt like her whole body was floating. Her head felt like it was spinning. Her heart was pounding. Her eyes couldn't stop staring, and her ears couldn't stop listening. But was all this really true? Mary heard something about a baby, something about being a mother, the Holy Spirit... She heard the name Jesus, Savior, Son of the Highest, the throne of David, a reign without end. Thousands of questions overwhelmed her. It was impossible to ask them all.

Little did Mary know what was going to happen in her life. There would be moments of fear and confusion, moments when nothing would make sense. God had chosen her; Mary would be the first to feel the Son of God. Infinite joy. "Blessed am I among all generations." A king would be born in a stable. Inconceivable. They would have to escape and hide. Their child would be lost, and then they would find a teacher. Admiration. Then miracles and inexplicable situations would come. The questions would continue for years. Persecution and more fear would come. Unexpected death would come. Confusion again. And again, life. Indestructible life this time. Complete joy.

Mary was still standing. Looking at that shining figure in front of her. Yes, she had many questions, and everything seemed very confusing to her. But one thing was clear:

"Here is the servant of the Lord; may He do with me as you say," she affirmed, determined.

Matthew 1:18-25; 2,
Luke 1:26-56; 2,
John 2:1-11; 19:25-27,
Acts 1:14

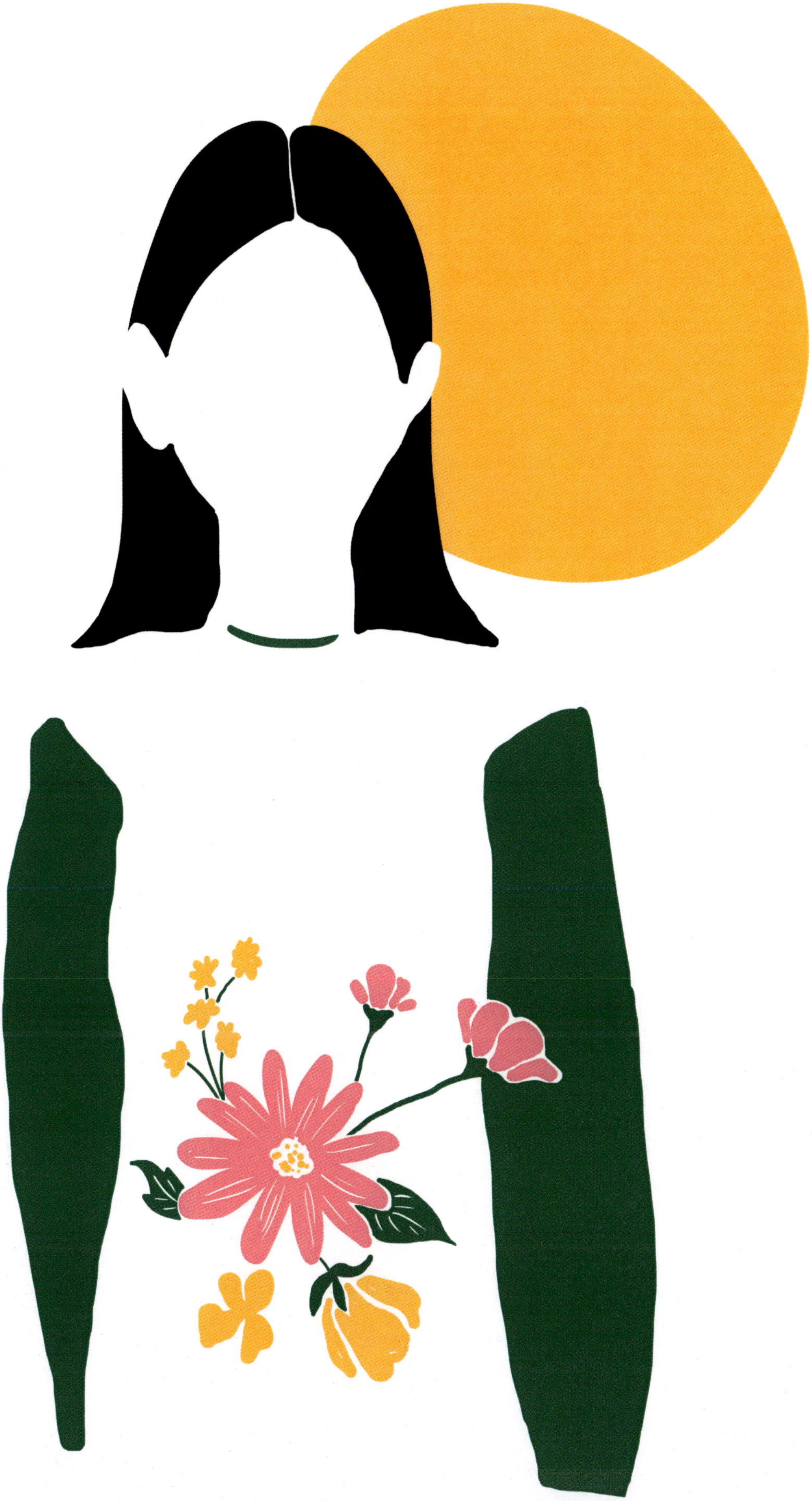

Elizabeth

Barely six months had passed since Zechariah, Elizabeth's husband, had received an angel of God announcement about the birth of their own son. God had managed to surprise them both. For years, they hadn't been able to have children, and now here was elderly Elizabeth with a growing belly that announced the birth of her baby. But that wasn't all; according to the angel, her son John, as he had commanded them to call him, would become a great man of God. Elizabeth had thought about this a lot during the last few months while resting in her house. She thought about what a great privilege she had to be able to give birth and see a servant of God grow up. But on that ordinary afternoon, Elizabeth did not know that God had even more surprises to reveal.

As soon as she heard her cousin's voice coming through the door, Elizabeth felt something suddenly move in her belly. This time it wasn't a slight kick like those she had begun to feel in recent days; her baby had just jumped for joy. It had been an intense movement like she had never experienced before. At that moment, the Holy Spirit flooded Elizabeth, and she had no doubt: her cousin Mary was also pregnant, and the baby she was expecting was the Messiah, the Christ who came to erase the pain and the mark of sin forever. She opened her mouth, and the words came out in a rush:

"Blessed are you, Mary, among all women, and blessed is your son. How is it possible that the mother of my Lord comes to visit me?"

There she was, in her own home. God had allowed her the privilege of being a mother, she was going to raise a man that God would use, and now, moreover, she was receiving Christ, the Savior of humanity, into her home. There would never be anyone greater than Him.

Elizabeth is described in the Bible as a woman of integrity, irreproachable and obedient to God. God is always looking for those who are willing to do His will, even in ways we can't even imagine.

Luke 1:5-24, 36-37, 39-66

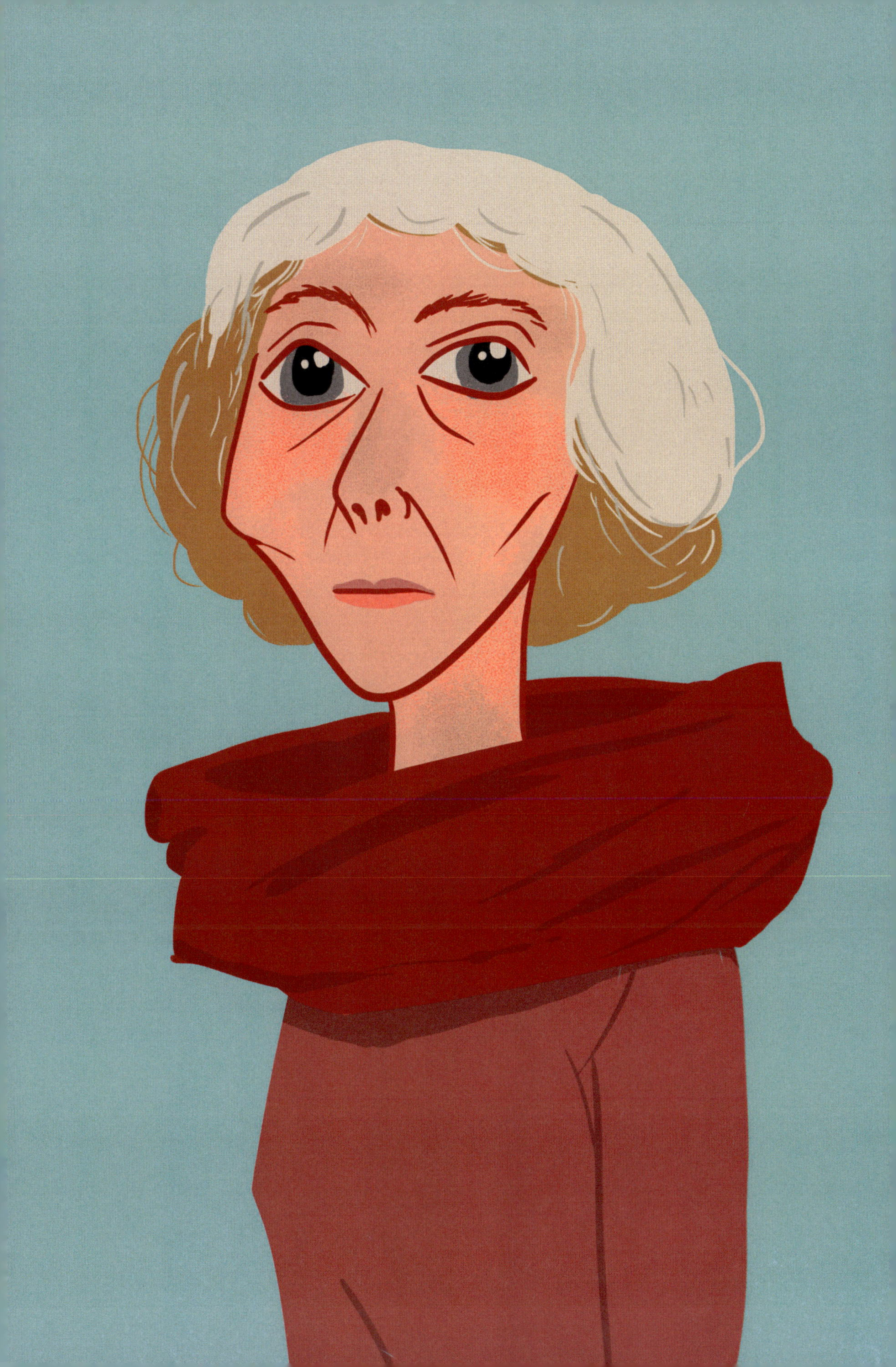

Anna

This is the story of Anna, a Jewish woman who belonged to the tribe of Asher. Anna married very young, but the death of her husband surprised her much sooner than expected. It was a hard blow, as it always is when someone we love leaves us unexpectedly. That could've been the start of a miserable life for Anna; her options as a widow in Israel were few. However, she decided to go ahead and find strength where she knew it abounded: in God.

Anna knew God well. God had spoken to her directly on several occasions to proclaim His message to others. She was a prophetess of God. When her husband died, Anna dedicated herself completely to worshiping God. Day and night, she stayed in the temple, the ancient stone building renovated by Herod the Great so that the people could draw closer to God. She prayed, fasted, and worshiped God there every single day. Because of her status as a woman, the temple authorities didn't allow her access to certain parts that other Jews could visit. But this didn't keep God from speaking directly to her, and she could speak to Him.

Years passed. Anna had spent most of her life as a widow within the temple walls, worshiping God day and night. She was already 84 years old and thought she had already seen everything. However, God had a big surprise in store for her.

Every day, new families brought their newborn children to the temple. The Jews had the custom of always presenting to God the first child born in a marriage. Joseph and Mary were carrying little Jesus, just a few weeks old. When Anna found out who Jesus was, she went over and, there, in the presence of everyone, raised her voice to God, giving thanks for the child and what His life meant to everyone. From that moment on, Anna didn't stop repeating that the Messiah had finally come to earth, encouraging all the people of Jerusalem who hoped that God would free His own, spreading hope in the hearts of those who listened to her.

Luke 2:36-38

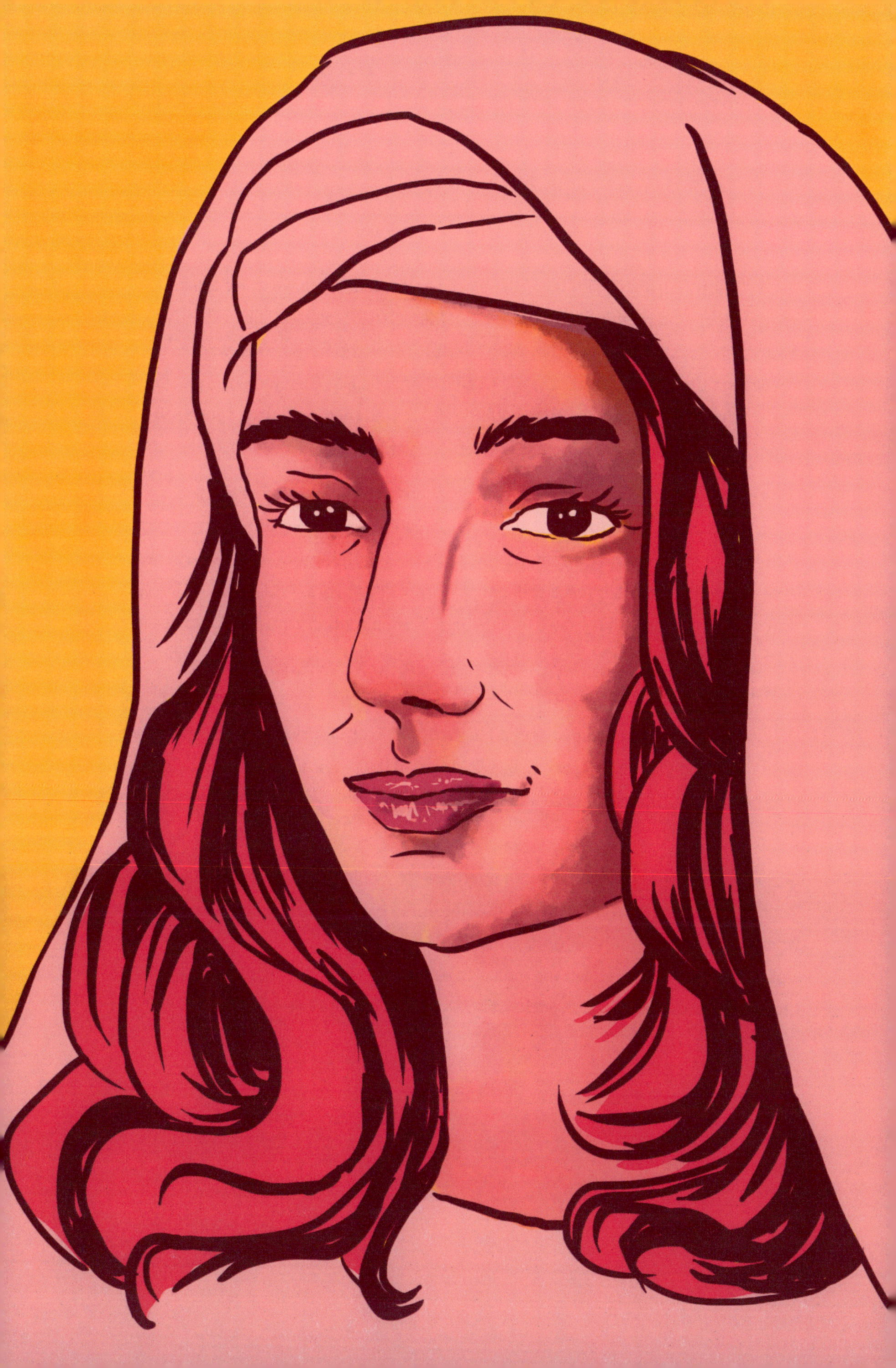

Susanna

Jesus began to walk from one place to another. As He went, He talked and taught things about God that they found hard to understand. People listened attentively to Him. Many were so impressed that they didn't want to return home; they just wanted to continue feeding on those words that seemed to give them life. But they weren't just words. Jesus had a unique way of reaching out to others. He treated them with love, spoke softly, looked them in the eyes, and made them feel loved, special.

This is how Susanna felt when Jesus approached her. Jesus looked at her and, in His eyes, Susanna felt a warm embrace. He took her hand, and when He did, all her fears disappeared. After a long time, Susanna felt safe, confident, as if everything around her was at peace. And that's when it happened; Jesus spoke that word. Only a word. And her affliction was gone forever. Suddenly. Nothing more was needed. A simple word from Jesus had been enough to put an end to such a long time of pain and despair. Susanna was herself again. Now, she was a healthy woman, a new woman — free at last.

Susanna smiled and stood up, relieved. Her body felt light, like it was floating above everyone else's. Everyone was looking at her. She could see in their expressions the astonishment that she herself felt. She could hardly believe it. Who was this who could do such things? She wasn't sure, but it didn't matter; something like this could only come from God.

Jesus started walking again. Who knew where He would go now? Who else would He heal along the way? What new words would come out of His mouth? No, Susanna wouldn't stand there watching Him leave. She adjusted her skirt and began to walk through the crowd that followed Him. From then on, she meant to never leave Him; she was determined to follow in His footsteps, to go wherever He went. She wouldn't miss one more of His words of life.

Luke 8:1-3

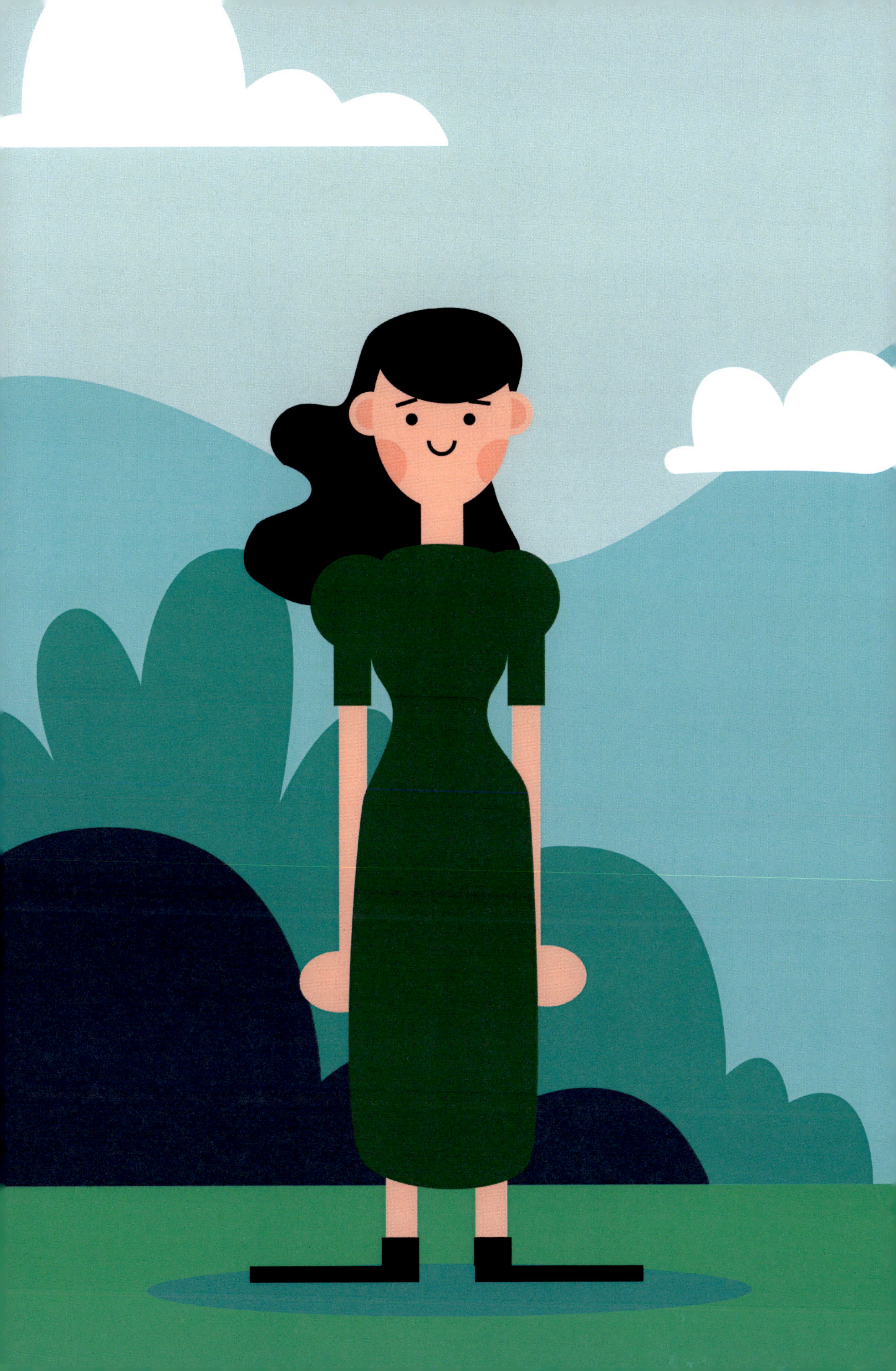

Joanna

Life in the palace of Herod Antipas was hectic and full of chores. Joanna moved through its corridors as if it were her own home. Floor-length curtains, fur-covered armchairs, gold and silver furniture, impressive porticoes, ponds with water flowing through bronze statues surrounded by abundant vegetation. Just a small taste of the king's power. Joanna's husband, Chuza, was in charge of administering all of Herod's possessions. He, better than anyone, knew the king's vast wealth and huge properties. The palace was always full of people. Servants who did their best to keep the power of their magnificent lord unshakeable. But also friends and followers who attended the many parties and banquets where they laughed, bragged, and made fun of others, such as the followers of a certain Jesus of Nazareth.

Joanna knew this Jesus. What she had heard about Him at the palace didn't correspond at all with reality. Jesus was powerful, unlike King Herod, whose power could disappear at any moment. The power of Jesus had always existed and would remain forever. Joanna cared little about the richness and the comfortable life she knew so well. She wanted to follow Jesus. It didn't matter if that closed the gates of Herod's palace to her forever. She wasn't sure how her husband would take it, either. She knew that her decision had important repercussions for his work as administrator of the king.

Joanna grabbed her bag. She put all her money in it, took some personal things, wore the most comfortable sandals she had, and left the palace, looking for Jesus. She would travel with the Master and His disciples from that day on. They would probably need money for the trip, and she was good at finding accommodation and arranging deals with suppliers. She knew of other women who were traveling with them as well. She was willing to give everything she had to the One who had completely changed her life.

Luke 8:1-3; 23:48-49, 55-56; 24:1-10

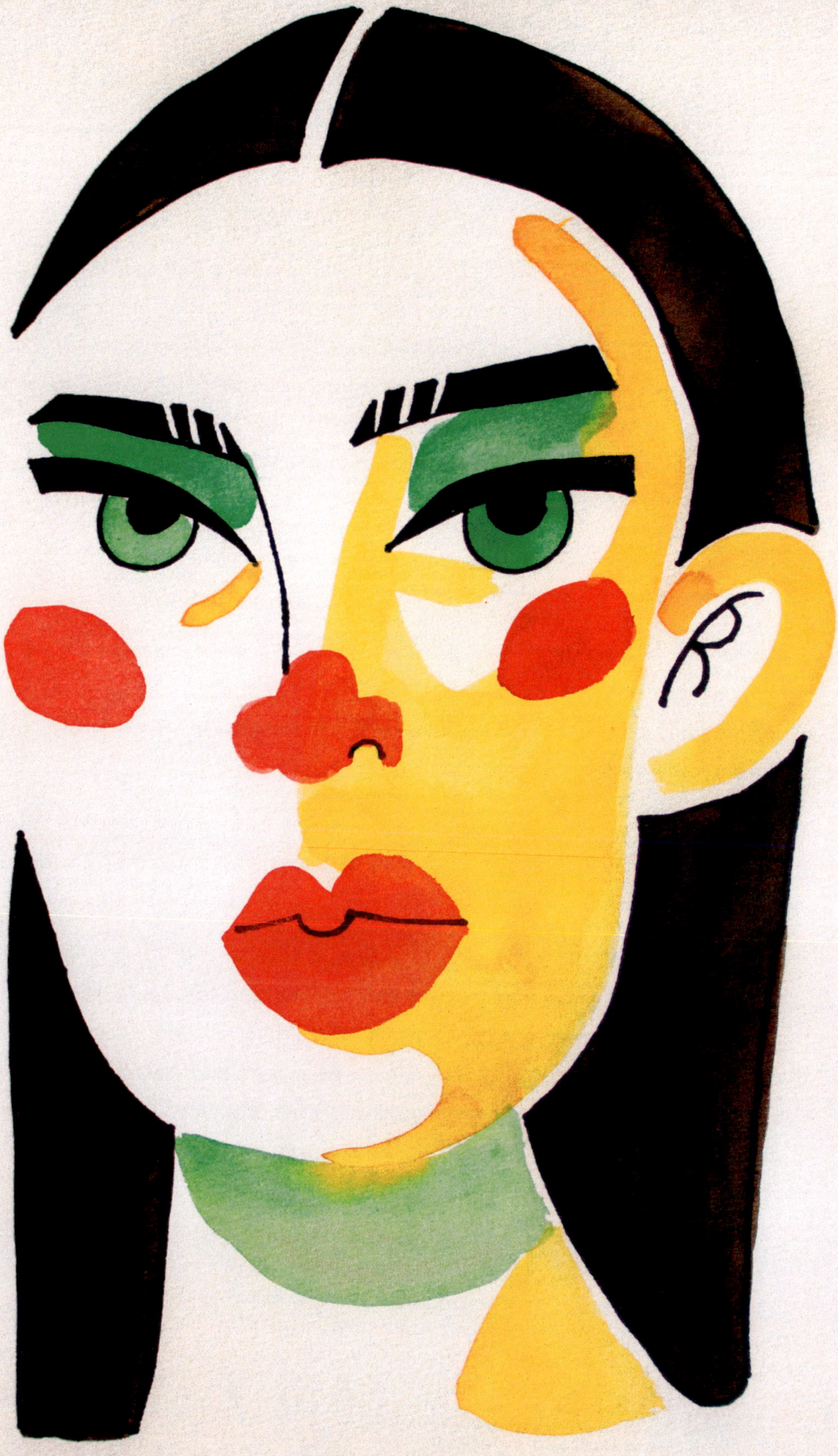

Martha

The village of Bethany, where Martha lived with her siblings, seemed larger than ever that day. Martha ran as tears streamed down her cheeks. She had heard that Jesus, a good family friend, was on His way. She had been waiting for Him for the last four days, ever since her brother Lazarus became very ill, and she, along with her sister Mary, decided to send someone to tell Him. Jesus had received the message, Martha was sure of it. But, contrary to what they expected, Jesus had not come. Now, their brother was dead. It had been a terrible few days. Martha, still running through the outskirts of Bethany, finally saw Jesus in the distance.

"Jesus!" she shouted almost breathlessly. "Why didn't You come before? You could have prevented his death."

Martha finally stopped. Unlike her, Jesus breathed slowly and remained calm. He looked at her with deep love. Martha knew how much He loved the three of them, so she didn't understand why Jesus hadn't answered her first call. Jesus asked Martha to keep her faith in Him; then, Martha left and ran back to the house again.

Jesus came a bit later. He approached the tomb and ordered it to be opened. Martha tried to stop Him; Lazarus had been dead for four days, so it was better not to open the tomb. Jesus looked her in the eyes and, again, reminded her to believe in Him. Martha saw His eyes. They were red, swollen, and wet. Jesus really loved them.

What happened next was so quick that Martha barely had time to react. Someone, following the order of Jesus, opened the tomb. Immediately afterward, Jesus began to pray and thanked God for always listening to Him. Then, to everyone's astonishment, Lazarus walked out. He was alive! After dying four days ago, Lazarus, her brother, was alive! Martha looked at Jesus. She looked back at Lazarus again. And once more, she looked at Jesus: without a doubt, nothing was impossible for Him.

Luke 10:38-42,
John 11:1-44

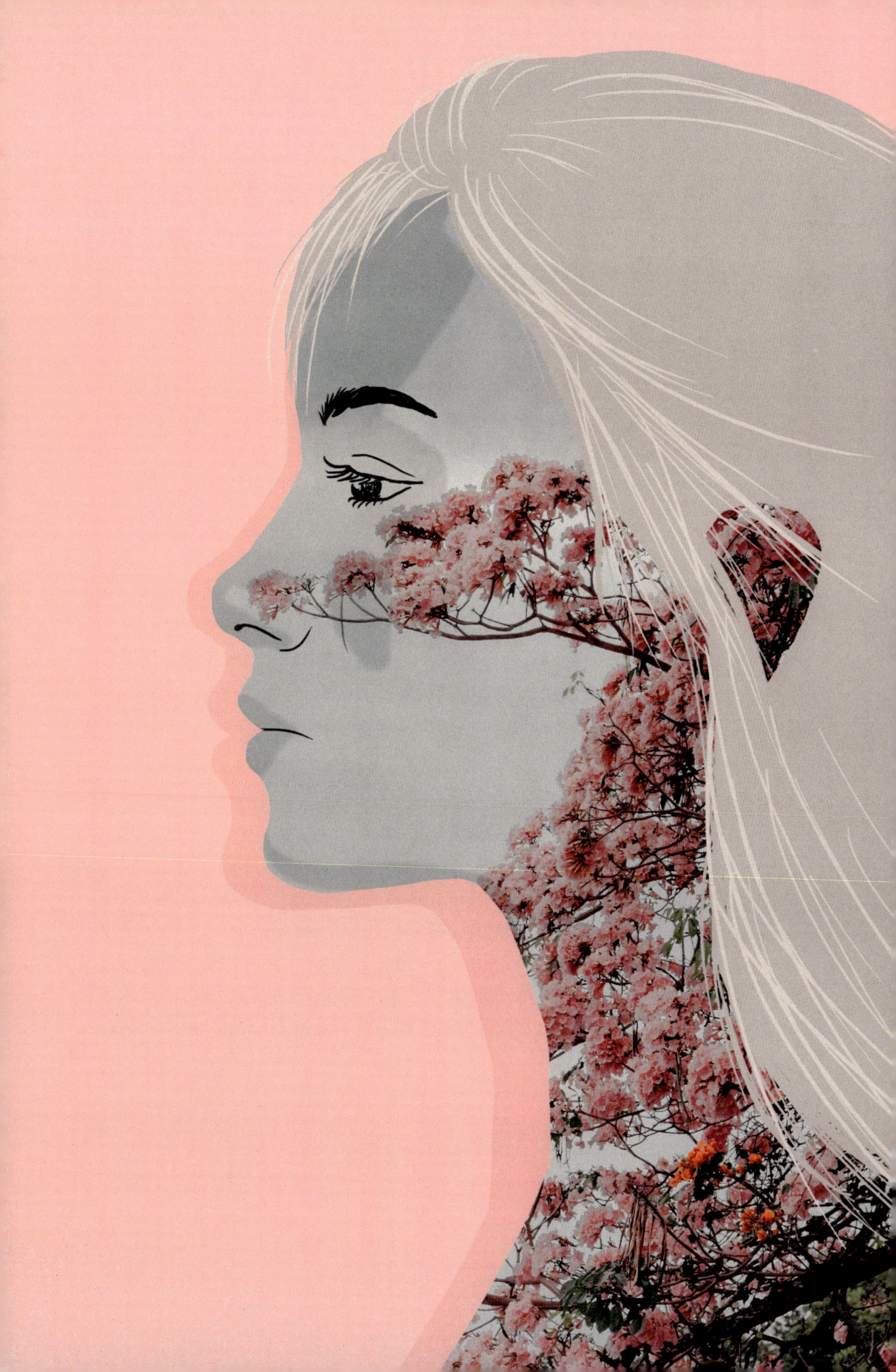

Mary of Bethany

The house of the three siblings was a "must-visit" every time Jesus passed through. Jesus loved Lazarus, Martha, and Mary in a special way; they always made room for Him there, and they loved to welcome Him. Martha, always so practical and perfectionistic, worked for hours so that everything was ready for the Master: the house very clean, the guest room prepared, the food ready. Mary, on the other hand, liked to wait patiently for His arrival, to breathe in the deep peace that always enveloped Jesus, and to sit at His feet to listen to Him speak. There was something special in the way He spoke. There was peace. There was wisdom. There was forgiveness.

In her hands, Mary held the bottle she had been keeping so carefully. She opened it and closed her eyes to smell its contents. Pure nard. The fresh smell of wood and spices that she loved so much. She had saved a good pint of that perfume for a special occasion. This was that occasion: a dinner in honor of Jesus. Lazarus had insisted on inviting Him that day. From the day Jesus had brought him back to life, he hadn't stopped thinking about that celebration. Not even the best banquet on earth would be enough to thank Jesus for what He had done for their family.

The voices of everyone at the table were animated and full of laughter. Mary came and knelt down next to the place where Jesus was. She opened the bottle again and slowly let the perfume fall on His tired feet, marked by sandals and long walks. Little by little, the liquid soaked Jesus' feet. In just a few seconds, the aroma of the nard's small whitish flowers filled the room. Mary continued pouring until there was not a single drop left in the bottle. Not paying too much attention, she heard the men talking, perhaps about money, the poor, a grave, but she continued to concentrate on what she was doing. She grabbed her long hair and used it, rubbing gently, to dry Jesus' feet, the feet that had brought forgiveness and hope to her life.

Luke 10:38-42,
John 11:1-12:7

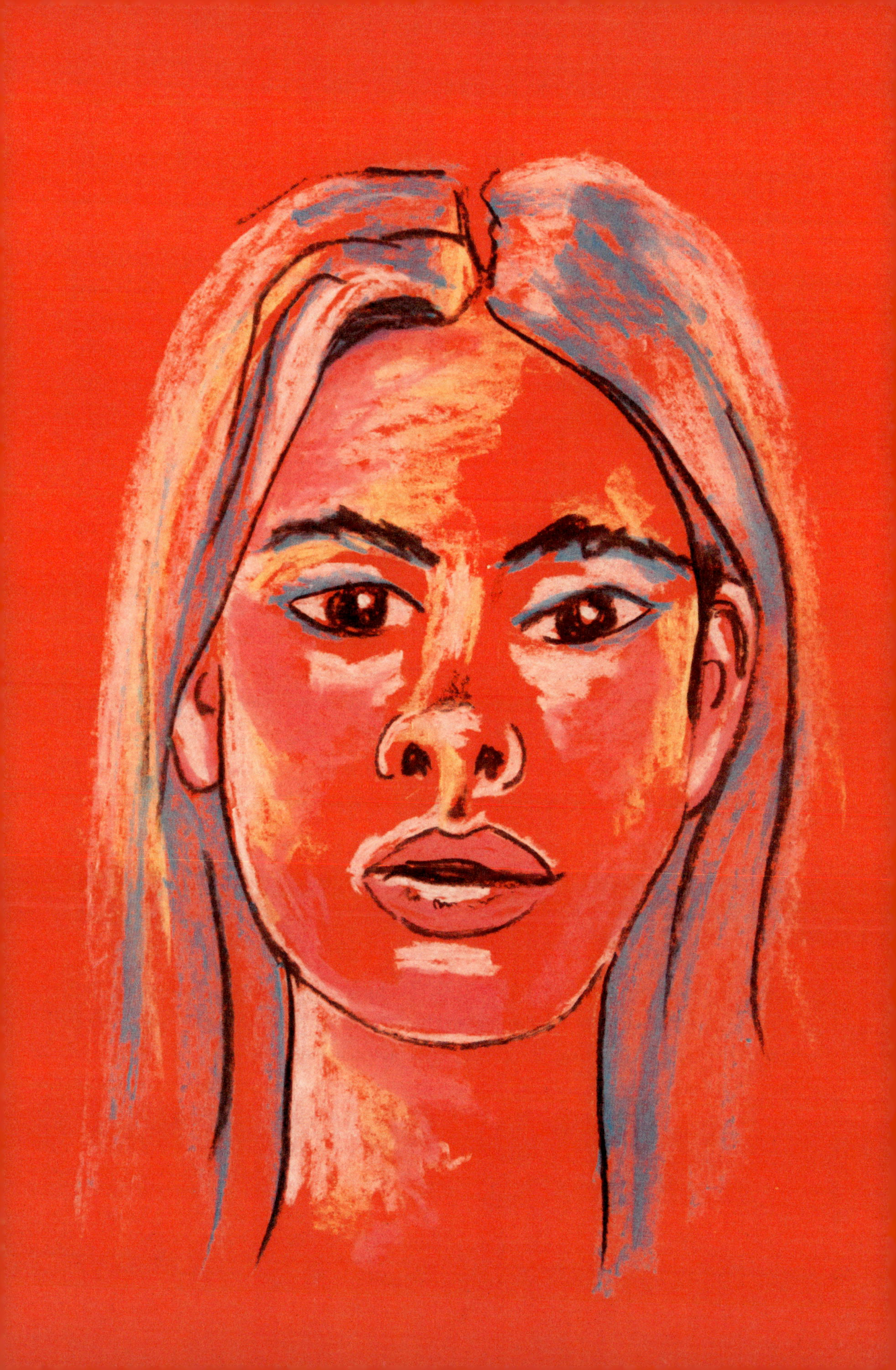

Salome

There were only a few hours left before the Passover meal began. Salome was radiant; that year, she had traveled with Jesus, His disciples, and some other women to Jerusalem to celebrate. It was a long journey from Galilee, and they had visited other cities along the way, but the excitement gave her energy. She was looking forward to everything that would happen during this year's celebration close to Jesus.

However, nothing turned out as expected. A series of unforeseen events twisted their plans, and suddenly, Salome found herself attending the execution of Jesus. It had all happened so fast. Salome still couldn't understand what they were accusing Him of, but somehow, Jesus had been sentenced to death. After beating and ridiculing Him, they hung Him on a cross.

Salome spent most of the day on Mount Golgotha. She saw Mary, the mother of Jesus, at the foot of the cross, but she herself couldn't get close. Her strength was failing her. She preferred to see everything from a distance, along with the other two Marys. She was so scared. She expected Jesus to come down off the cross at any moment as if nothing had happened. But He did nothing to end His own suffering. Nor did He lament or speak out against those who had put Him there. Salome didn't lose sight of His face, full of pain; she realized that little by little, He was feeling weaker and weaker.

As she watched Him breathe heavily, Salome remembered all the moments she had lived with Him. She thought of the times He had approached her. She remembered the sweet expression on His face, His firm but loving voice. She looked at the other women out of the corner of her eye. Tears fell from their eyes. No one said anything. There was nothing to say.

Suddenly, Jesus cried out for the last time. The sky turned dark. An earthquake shook the earth. The people gave a terrified shriek, and then there was absolute silence. Salome saw fear on the faces of the crowd. She already knew it, though many did not: truly, Jesus was the Son of God.

Mark 15:40-41; 16:1-8,
Luke 23:55-56

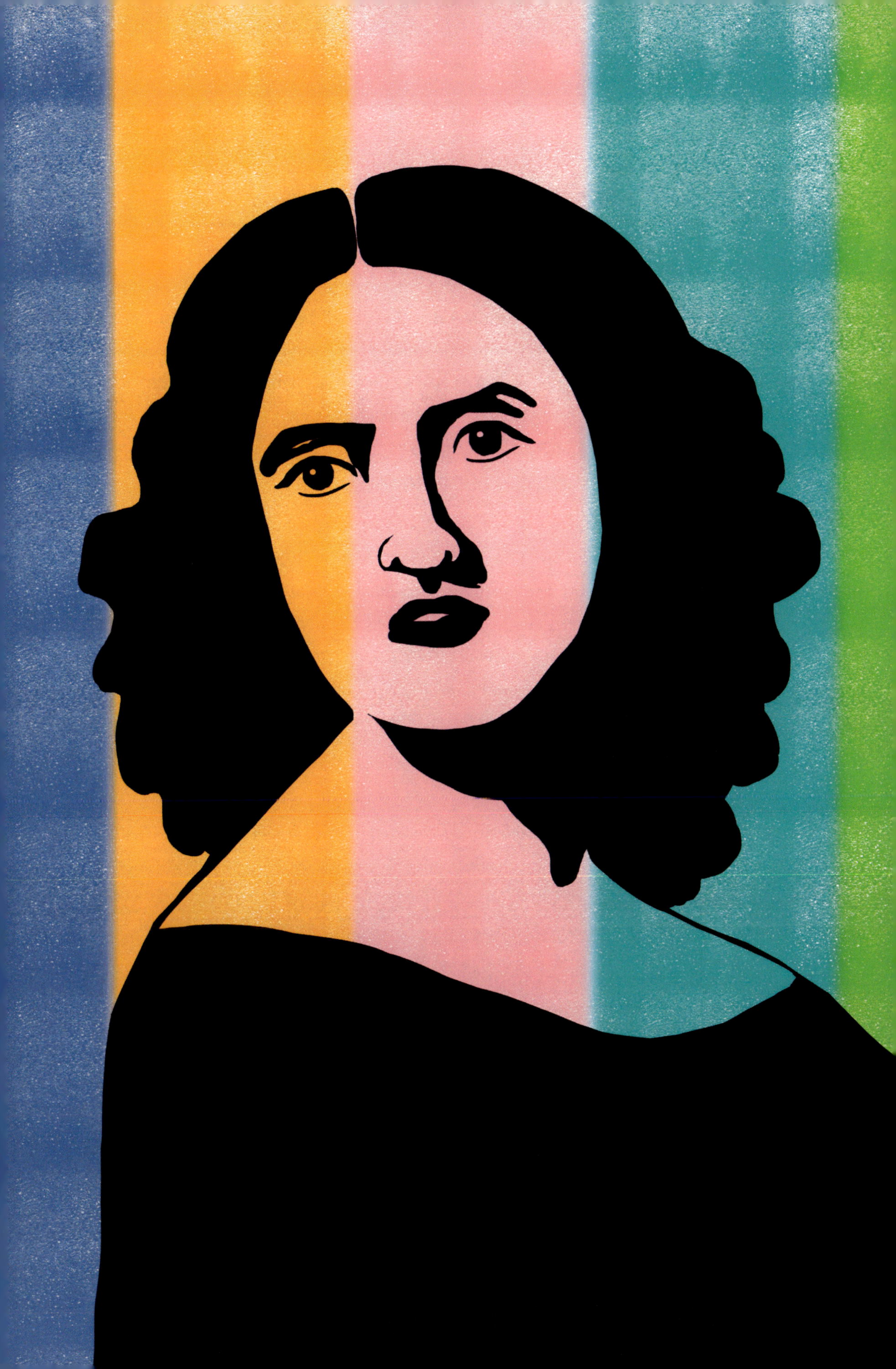

Mary of Galilee

It had been an intense day. Mary felt as though she were about to faint due to the many emotions she experienced during the day. She hadn't been able to talk about it yet with her children — surely they were with the rest of the disciples — but Jesus was dead. Mary had seen it all with her own eyes. The rest of the women who had accompanied Him from Galilee were also witnesses. They had seen how they put the body of Jesus in a tomb. They had stayed there together, with their arms wrapped around each other, until they saw the closed tomb closed, covered with a very heavy stone.

Then one of the women realized something. They hadn't even had time to bury Him! For the Jews, this was something very important. When someone died, they honored the body by covering it with ointments and perfumes. Immediately, Mary and the rest rushed out to look for spices and perfumes with which to anoint the body of Jesus. They ran to get everything ready before Saturday arrived. Jewish law didn't allow them to do anything on the Sabbath, so they would have to wait until the next morning, the first day of the week, to go to the tomb and properly embalm Jesus. They would then have to figure out how to remove the stone covering the tomb.

Mary tried to get some rest that night. She managed to get a little, but she was still exhausted by Saturday morning. She had the whole day ahead of her. A silent and dark day where the hours barely seem to pass. Time to reflect and ask questions that perhaps would never have an answer. Was this how it all ended? Was death reigning again? Hopelessness and darkness, just like before she met Him.

But what Mary didn't know yet was that it was all part of the plan. God kept working, even when she couldn't see it. Jesus was not finished. And very soon, as soon as the sun announced the dawn, life would be visible to all.

Matthew 27:55-56, 61; 28:1,
Mark 15:40, 47; 16:1-19,
Luke 8:2; 24:10;
John 19:25; 20:1-8

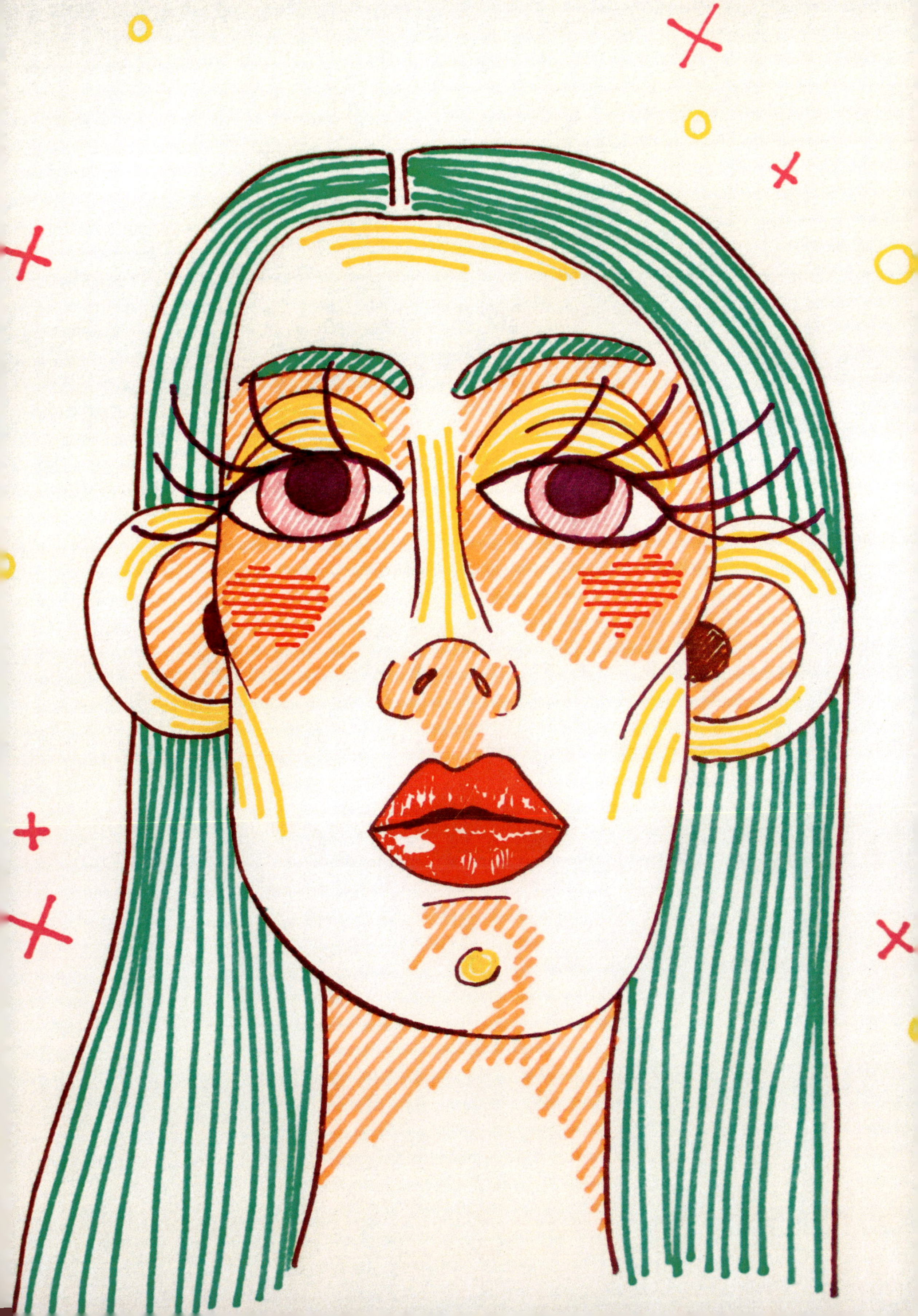

Mary of Magdala

Her name was Mary, although everyone knew her as Mary Magdalene in honor of her hometown, Magdala. She had had a difficult life. She had made wrong decisions and put herself in danger. That's why her health had been severely affected. But all this was the past. She met Jesus, and that changed her entire life. Since then, she had joined a group of disciples and other followers who traveled with Him.

However, in the last few hours, nothing seemed to make sense. Jesus had been crucified and buried; and, if that weren't enough, now his body was missing. She had discovered the tomb open and completely empty when she arrived early that morning. She quickly warned the disciples. Peter and John came running to check it out, too. She felt desperate. Who would have dared to do something so terrible?

The disciples had left; they would all be gathered to see what they could do. Mary Magdalene cried inconsolably at the tomb of her Lord. Then she peeked in again. But this time, she saw something different. Two angels were sitting on the place where Jesus' body should be. She turned around, and another figure suddenly appeared before her eyes. At first, she found it hard to believe, but after a few seconds, she realized it was Jesus, speaking and smiling as always.

"Teacher!" Mary cried in shock.

She was the chosen one. A woman with a past full of mistakes and sin. Jesus had chosen her. Out of thousands of men and women, many of them with more merits and better positions, Jesus wanted her to be the first to see His resurrected body. The first to know the message of eternal life. The first to know of the triumph of life over sin and death. Jesus had also chosen her as the one to announce it to all the others.

Matthew 27:55-56, 61; 28:1-10,
Mark 15:40, 47; 16:1-11,
Luke 8:1-3; 24:1-10,
John 19:25; 20:1-8

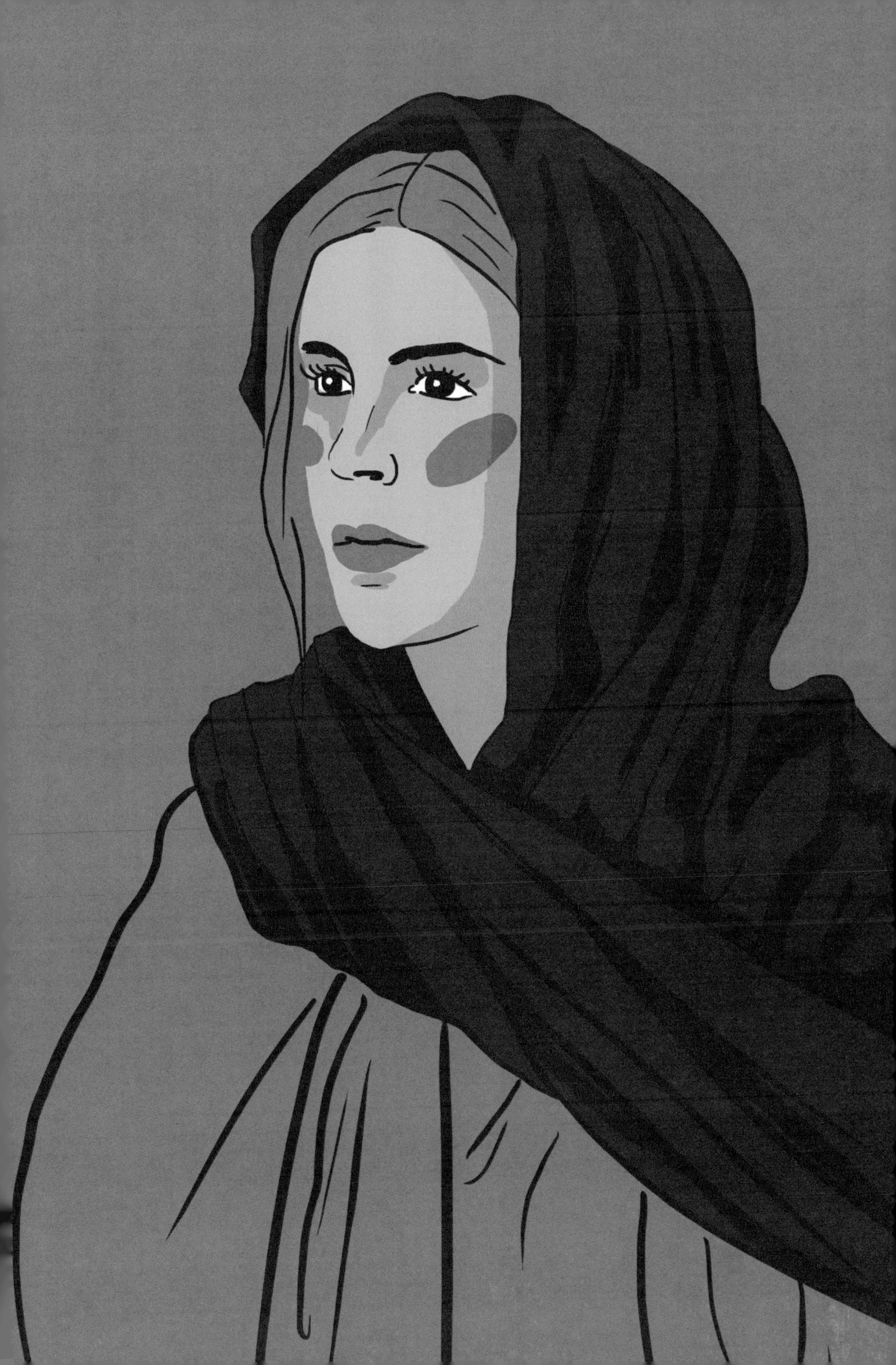

Tabitha

Joppa was a coastal city on the shores of the Mediterranean Sea. Many there knew Tabitha, a disciple completely dedicated to God's service. Every day she could be seen sewing at the entrance of her house. She made robes and dresses to give to anyone who needed them. Many widowed women in Joppa wore her clothes gratefully. Many poor people also knew her because she had brought them something warm or hot food to eat on a cold night. With her endearing motherly love, she attended to the needs of others as if they were her own family. Her hands never stopped working for the good of those most in need. That's why she was so loved in Joppa.

But one day, Tabitha fell seriously ill. Everyone who knew her felt sad, and even more so when they received the news that Tabitha had died. Many people gathered to mourn her absence. She had helped so many! A disciple then suggested that they have Peter come. Everyone had heard the latest news: Peter had healed a paralyzed man in Lydda, a city close by. Two men ran out to look for him.

When Peter arrived at Tabitha's house, he found a large crowd. The disciples were there waiting for him. Many women cried over Tabitha's death. They showed Peter the dresses that she had sewn for them. They all started talking at the same time; each one told him how much Tabitha had helped them when they were in need.

Peter entered the room where Tabitha's body was. He got down on his knees and prayed for a while. Then, turning to Tabitha, he asked her to get up. Immediately she opened her eyes, looked at Peter, and sat up in bed. Peter extended his hand and helped her to stand up.

When the other disciples saw her standing, they worshiped God because of the miracle. The widows began to shout for joy. The news quickly spread throughout the city. Tabitha had helped many in Joppa, but that day, even more believed in the Lord because of what God had done in her life.

Acts 9:36-42

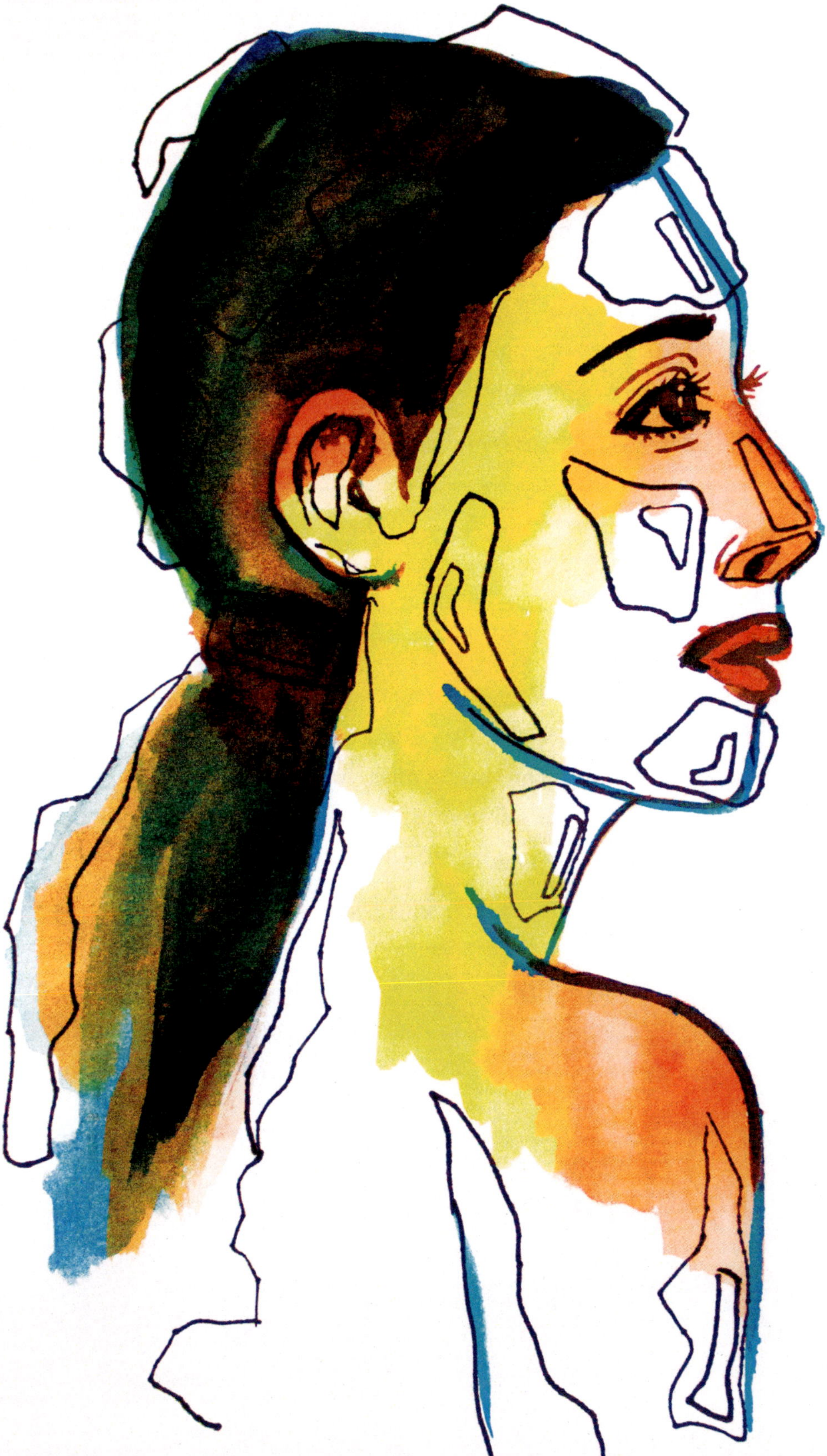

Mary of Jerusalem

Her family may have come from Cyprus, but her heart was in Jerusalem, where she had lived for some time. There in Jerusalem, she saw how her little Mark became a faithful follower of Jesus. Mary knew this was the best path to follow, not only for her son but also for herself. It was true that Jesus was no longer with them physically, but His teachings continued to spread from one follower to another.

Mary knew that many Christians in Jerusalem were afraid. After Jesus left, Herod had tried to finish off all His followers. Mary thought that wouldn't be easy, but the king's efforts irritated her. Herod didn't like Christians; he thought he was the only authority in Jerusalem and wouldn't let the people follow anyone else. He had already arrested and hurt some of them. But the Christians stood firm on the teachings of Jesus. Nothing would change their minds.

The doors of Mary's house were open for the Christians to gather. It was a fairly large house, so Mary thought they would be comfortable there. She felt privileged to open her doors and worship alongside others who had found hope for their lives, just as she had. She liked to see them come and fill the rooms of her house. She knew it was dangerous; if the authorities found out about it, she would be in trouble, but still, she was willing to take the risk.

Jerusalem's church was the first church to be formed. It was a very important group of Christians. From there, many traveled to surrounding cities to preach to others. This is how many other churches were formed. Thanks to her service to the Christians of Jerusalem, Mary had the privilege of God using her house to welcome this group of His children who in turn spread to all the surrounding cities.

Acts 12:12

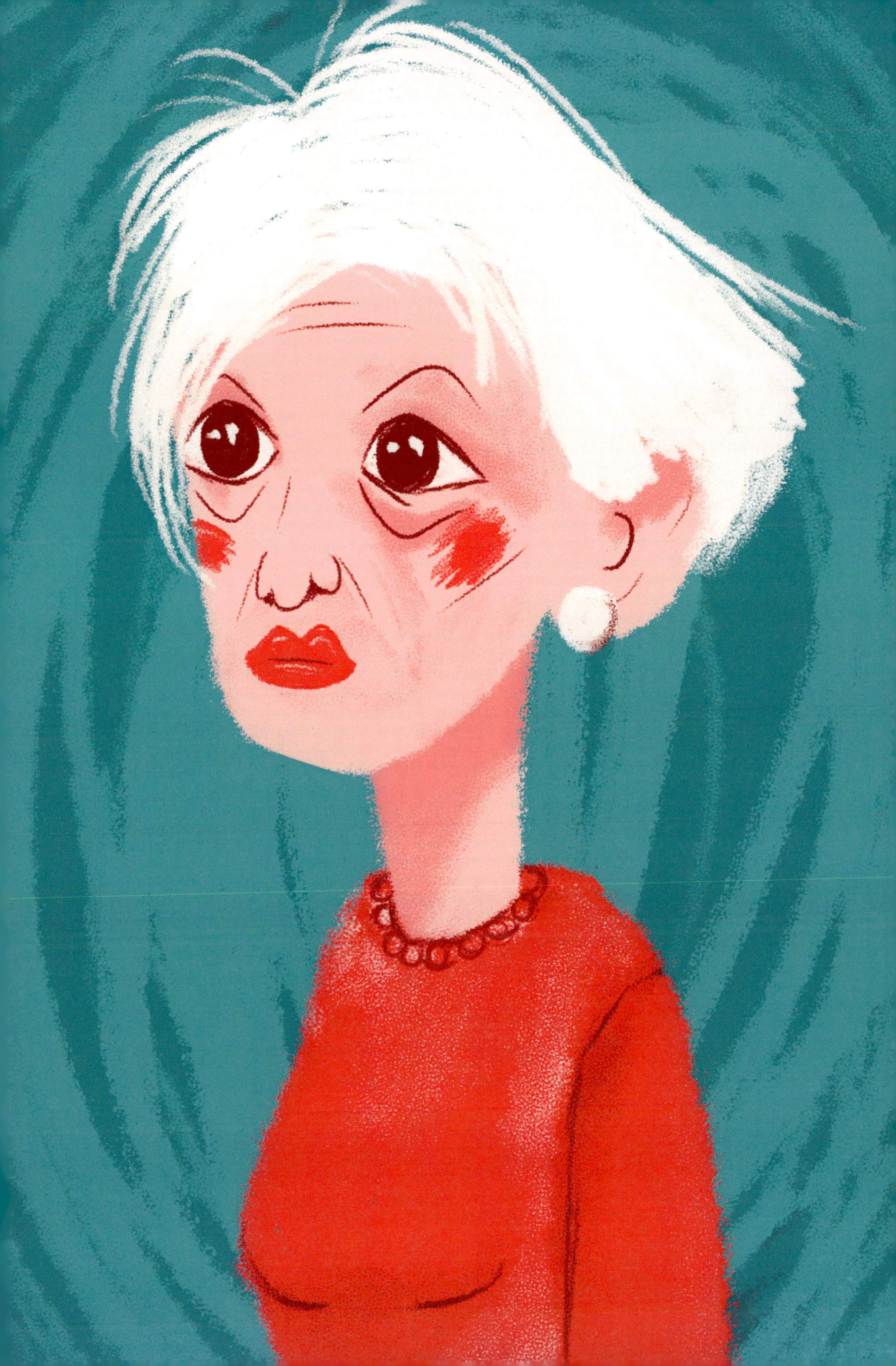

Rhoda

It was late, but the Christians in Jerusalem were not going home just yet. That same night, Herod Agrippa had summoned the trial to convict Peter, whom he had arrested just a few days before.

Rhoda watched nervously as the group prayed asking God to deliver Peter from death. She had heard that Herod wanted to kill Peter, as he had already done with James. Many were gathered at Mary's house to pray, the house where Rhoda worked as a maid. They had been getting together to do the same thing for days. They begged God to hear their prayers. They asked for Peter's freedom. Some asked Him to be with Peter and give him strength during difficult times. Others prayed that God would give him the right words to defend himself in court. Someone mentioned a miracle.

"Yes, God, perform a miracle."

Someone knocked on the door. Rhoda thought it would be some other Christian straggler coming to pray too. She knew that she couldn't open the door to just anyone; the Roman authorities were looking for Christians to arrest them, and she wouldn't want them to be discovered there. Before opening the door, she asked who it was. Listening to the voice on the other side of the door, her ears couldn't believe what they heard. That voice. Yes, it was, without a doubt, Peter's voice. Peter was there! Somehow, he had gotten out of jail, and he was right there! Rhoda jumped up and, forgetting to open the door, immediately ran into the living room, where everyone was praying.

"Peter is at the door!" she yelled, breaking the silence in the room.

Everyone immediately looked at her. There was a moment of silence. Nervous, Rhoda nodded insistently as Peter continued to knock impatiently on the door. Some, hardly believing, looked at each other. Finally, someone got up and went to open the door. Peter ran in. It was really him! Rhoda looked at him with immense joy. God definitely answers prayers.

Acts 12:13-16

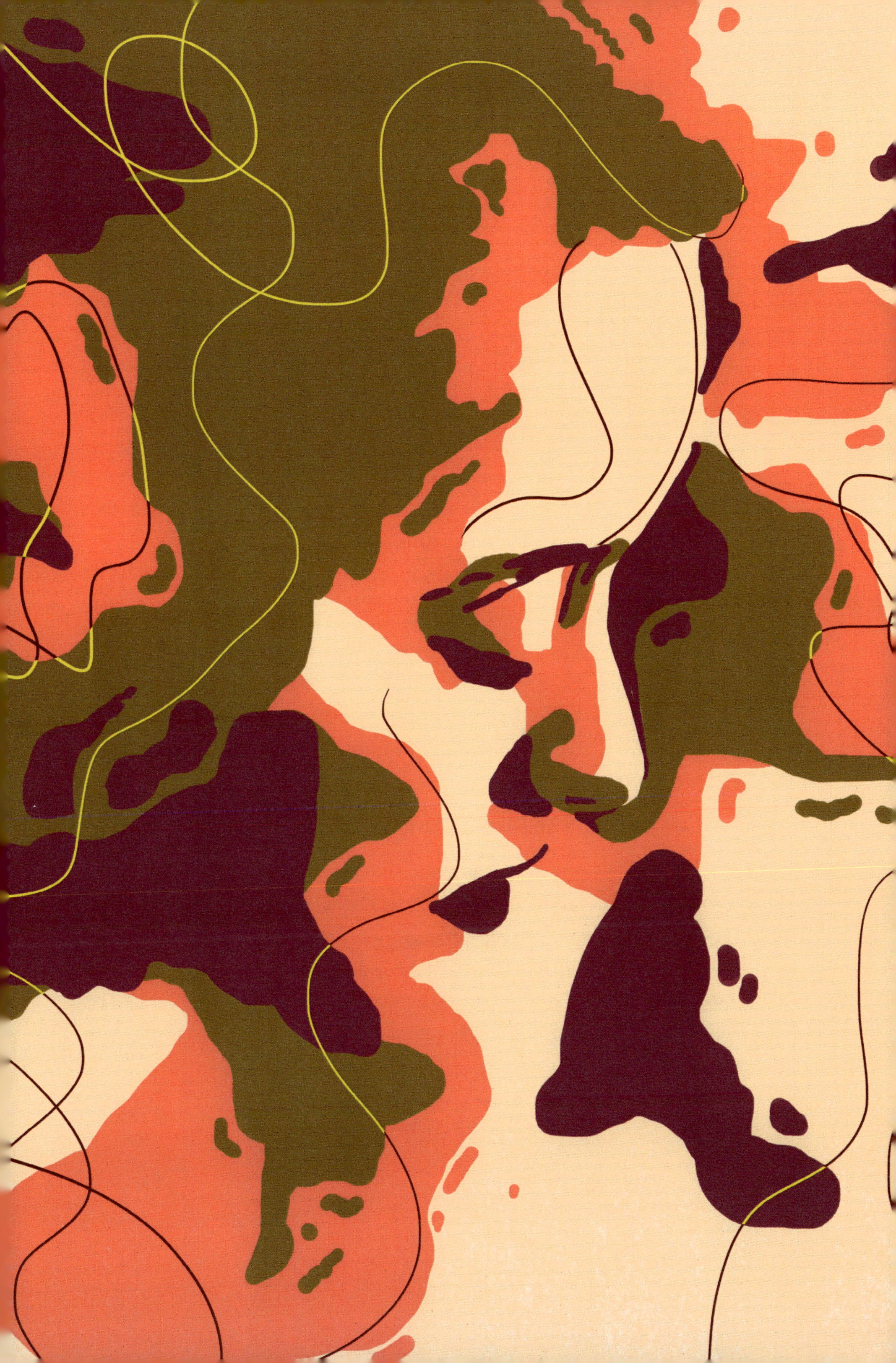

Lydia

On the Asian continent, in a place that today is part of Turkey, there was once a city famous for its dyes called Thyatira. Many of its citizens worked at dyeing fabrics. Among them was Lydia, a distinguished woman who had learned to dye purple, a very expensive dye used by wealthy and powerful people.

Lydia decided to move to Europe and went to Philippi, where she met many wealthy people who bought her cloth. There were not many people from her country in Philippi, but she made friends with other foreigners: people of Jewish origin. By spending time with them, Lydia learned more about their culture and history and took a special interest in their God. Lydia liked to get together with other Jewish women every Saturday to worship God. In Philippi, the Jews didn't have a synagogue where they could meet, so they met on the riverbank outside the city.

One day, some men came to where the women were gather to pray and worship God. The man began to talk to them about Jesus. All this was new to Lydia, but she was impressed by the words of a man named Paul. That day, God opened Lydia's heart, and she decided that she would be a Christian from then on and was baptized immediately. Lydia was so happy that she told Paul and his companions:

"If you really consider me a Christian now, come to my house and stay there for a few days."

But Lydia opened the doors to her house much more than that, and a short time later, it was at her house that the newly founded church of Philippi began to meet. Lydia's house church became a very important church in the early years of Christianity. But in addition to contributing so importantly to the founding of this church, Lydia is remembered for being the first person in all of Europe to convert to Christianity. This is even more surprising not only because she wasn't Jewish but also because she was a woman. Thanks to Lydia, many others met Jesus as well.

Acts 16:14-15, 40

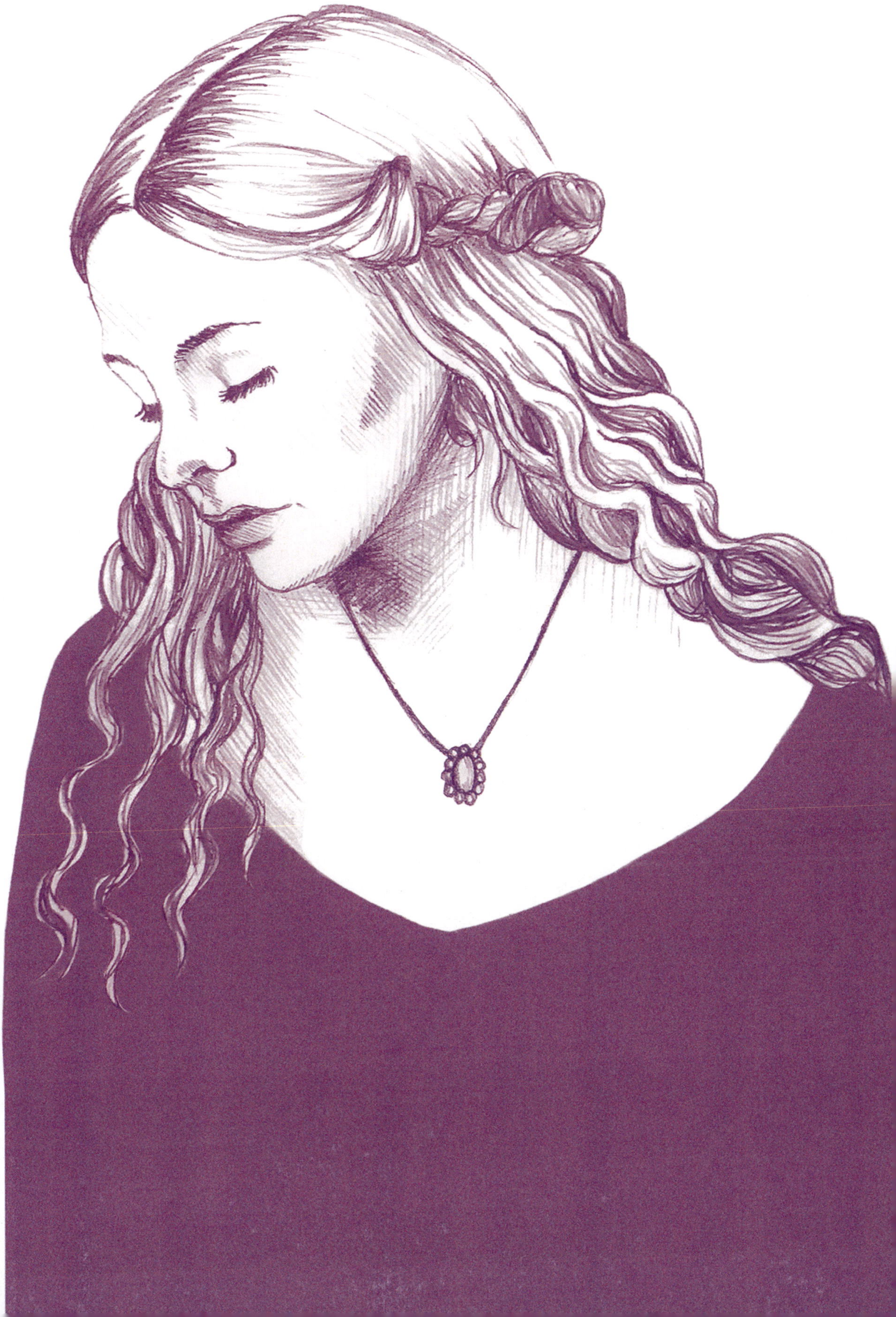

Damaris

Many years ago in Athens there lived a woman named Damaris. Back then, Greece was a country full of gods that people continually tried to please. They thought that they would suffer terribly if the gods were angry with them. For this reason, the country's cities were full of temples with statues. People would come before these statues to perform a series of rituals to avoid being punished by the gods.

One day, Damaris witnessed an argument that changed her life. A group of philosophers had brought a man to the Areopagus. The Areopagus was a group of judges that were in charge of solving any conflict that occurred in the city. The philosophers seemed very angry about some things that this man, Paul, had been saying in the square. Damaris was one of the few women present at a meeting like this, but she was immediately captivated by the conversation between the men. The philosophers accused Paul of being a babbler. Paul kept talking about some very strange things: about a God who had created everything that existed and didn't need humans. Damaris couldn't believe what she was hearing; she could've never imagined that something like this was possible. Paul continued talking about this God who was near and wanted everyone to find Him. A strong desire began to grow within Damaris: a close God, unlike the Greek gods everyone feared.

But suddenly, Paul spoke of a man whom God had resurrected. That was unbelievable! At that moment, there was a big stir. Many began to shout and make fun of Paul, and he had to flee from the meeting. Damaris didn't want him to leave. If this God existed, she had to find Him. He wasn't like the Greek gods she had heard so much about. He was different. Damaris ran out to look for Paul. It didn't matter if people made fun of her too or treated her badly for being a woman meddling in men's business, or even tried to hurt her. She needed to know this God. Despite everything, she was willing to be a Christian. And she followed Paul until she finally got to talk to him.

Acts 17:34

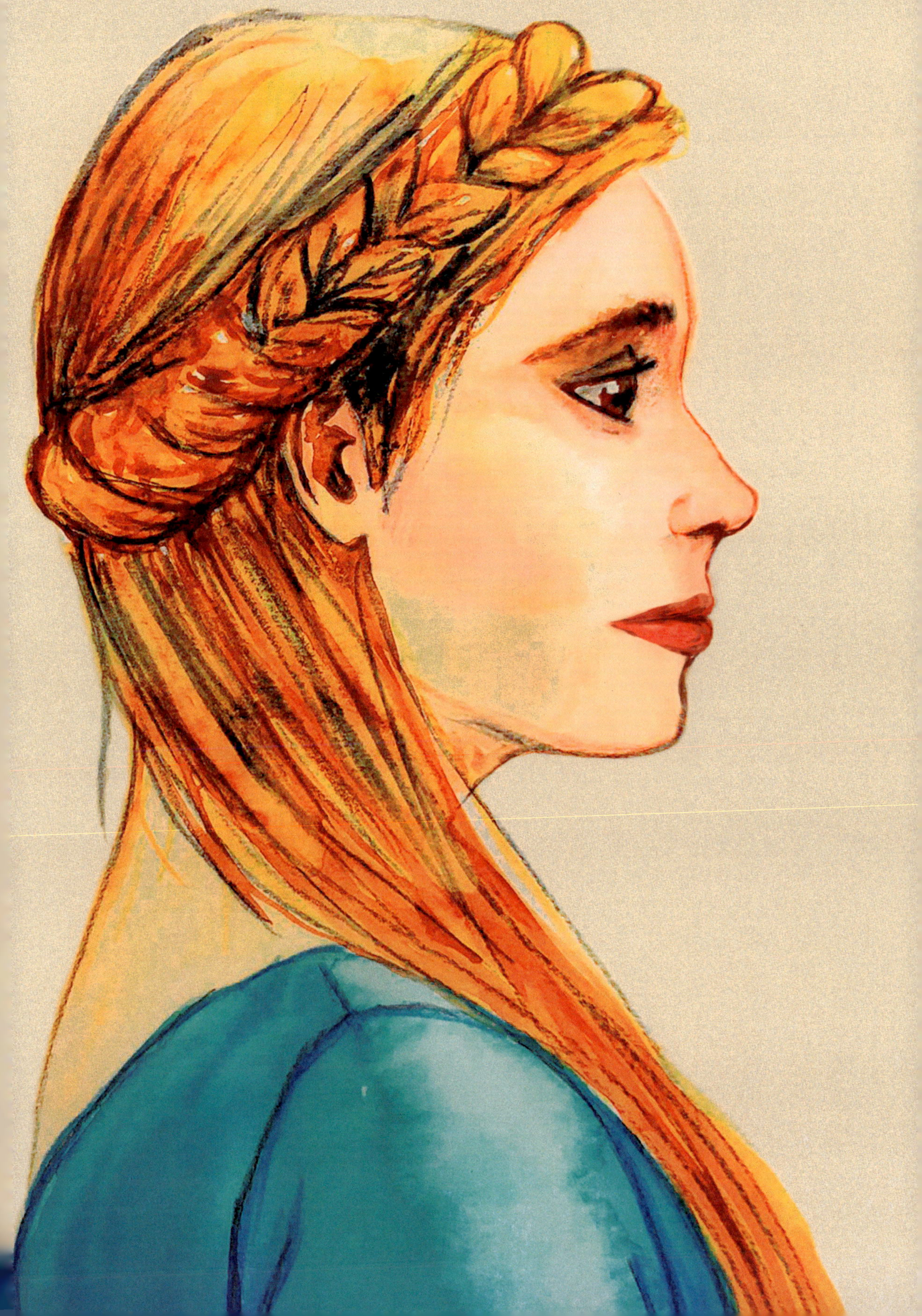

Priscilla

Prisca, affectionately called Priscilla by her friends, was a Jewish woman who lived in Rome with her husband, Aquila. Both worked together building tents until one day, the emperor of Rome, Claudius, imposed a law that forced the Jews to leave Rome. Among the Jews who had to leave were Priscilla and her husband.

Although it seemed inconvenient and unexpected, God had a plan for them. They settled in Corinth, where they started over. There, they continued with their career, they met new people, and God used them for His ministry. Among their new friends was Paul, another tent builder who decided to dedicate his life to making Jesus known to others. Priscilla and her husband invited him to their house, and not only him but the entire church of Corinth, who found a place to meet there. They also accompanied Paul and traveled with him, spreading the news of Jesus' death and resurrection to others.

Priscilla and her husband worked together in everything they did and were an example to others. They cared about the people around them and showed their love to each one, studying the scriptures with them, explaining the gospel, encouraging and strengthening new Christians, and being an example to others in the church. Once, they even risked their own lives to save Paul. Their work, dedication, and commitment to the gospel greatly impacted the churches of that time and even left a mark that has been reflected in some parts of the Bible that we can read today. The example of their marriage teaches us not only what it means to be a Christian but how to live lives that reflect what it is to be a true Christian.

Acts 18:2, 18, 26; Romans 16:3,4; 1 Corinthians 16:19; 2 Timothy 4:19

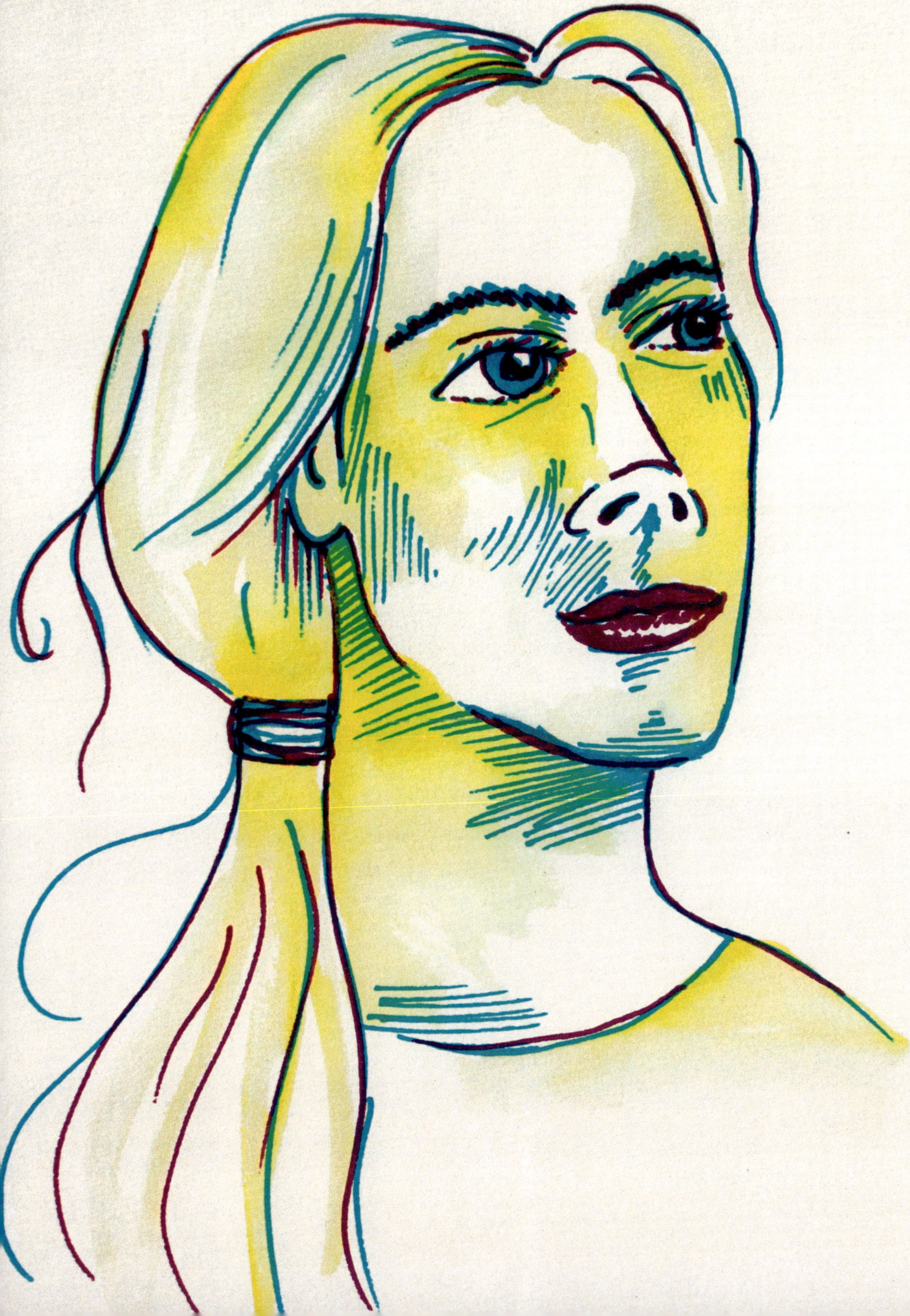

Chloe

A new morning began in Corinth. Chloe had just woken up and was about to sit by the window to eat breakfast. As she served herself, she remembered the conversation at home the night before. She had gone to bed thinking about it, and apparently, it was still on her mind. She was concerned about some issues that caused arguments among Christians.

Sometimes, being a Christian was a bit difficult. Some current matters generated confusion. Many Corinthian Christians still knew very little about God and Jesus and had only recently begun their new lives as Christians. Also, Corinth was a difficult place to be a Christian; people there generally behaved in a way that was not pleasing to God. Many new Christians in the church were still struggling to let go of some of their old behaviors. Some would be easier to abandon, but others would be much harder. They needed help from other more experienced Christians. The support and good example of other brothers and sisters can be a great help, especially when we go through more difficult times. But in the Corinthian church, sometimes some Christians would argue and get angry about what they saw instead of helping. They had formed small groups, and some refused to recognize others as brothers and sisters in Christ. Their main goal had become to argue about everything they disagreed on.

Chloe knew that the church would not get very far if they continued like this. Jesus had made it clear that love for others should be their main task. How much more so when those others were brothers and sisters of the church. They had to stop causing division and begin to grow and bear fruit as a church. They needed help. Perhaps what they had been talking about the day before was true, and they had to let Paul know so that he could come and lend a hand as soon as possible. Yes, it was clear they needed help.

1 Corinthians 1:11

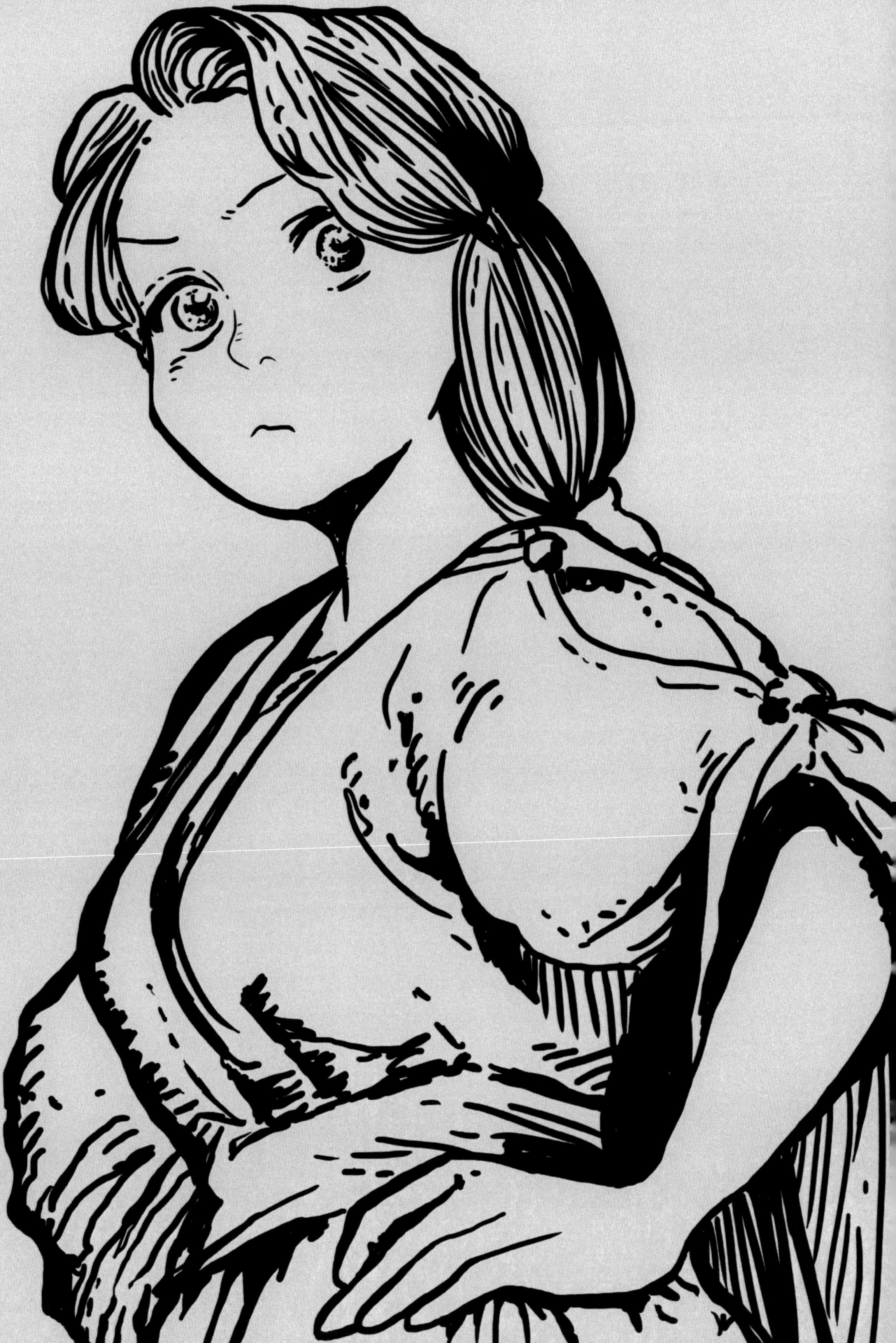

Phoebe

Cenchreae was a small maritime town very close to Corinth. Every day a large number of ships departed and arrived with travelers and provisions to be distributed to all the surrounding cities. That day, Phoebe was taking a ship to travel to Rome. Rome was a much larger city than her well-known Cenchreae; Phoebe would miss the town's narrow streets, the neighbors' closeness, and especially her beloved church during her trip. It was a small group of Christians, but Phoebe loved them in a special way. During her time away, she would miss working for God in the church as she did every week. Phoebe served as a deaconess; her heart was always ready to help other brothers and sisters and lend a hand when needed.

As she waited for the ship to sail for the empire's capital, she wondered what the church in Rome would be like. She had heard Paul talk about this congregation, much larger than her own. Paul had told her that she didn't have to worry about anything and that the brothers and sisters there would help her with whatever she needed during her stay in Rome. She and Paul had seen each other and talked just a few days ago because Paul had written a letter to the church of Rome that he wanted Phoebe to take and hand deliver.

Phoebe opened her bag and, after verifying that the papyrus was inside it, rolled tight and safe from being crushed by anything, she closed it again. She knew this letter was very important to Paul; he cared for churches all over the place. What a great example he was for all Christians! Although she didn't know them yet, she knew that her brothers and sisters in Rome would appreciate being able to read the words Paul had written for them. Phoebe was happy to be able to bring them that gift. Little did Phoebe imagine that, at that time, in her hands, God had entrusted a message not only to a group of Christians but to millions and millions of other people. In the centuries to come, those words written by Paul would be read by many in numerous cities worldwide, in countless congregations, and in hundreds of languages totally unknown to her.

Romans 16:1, 2

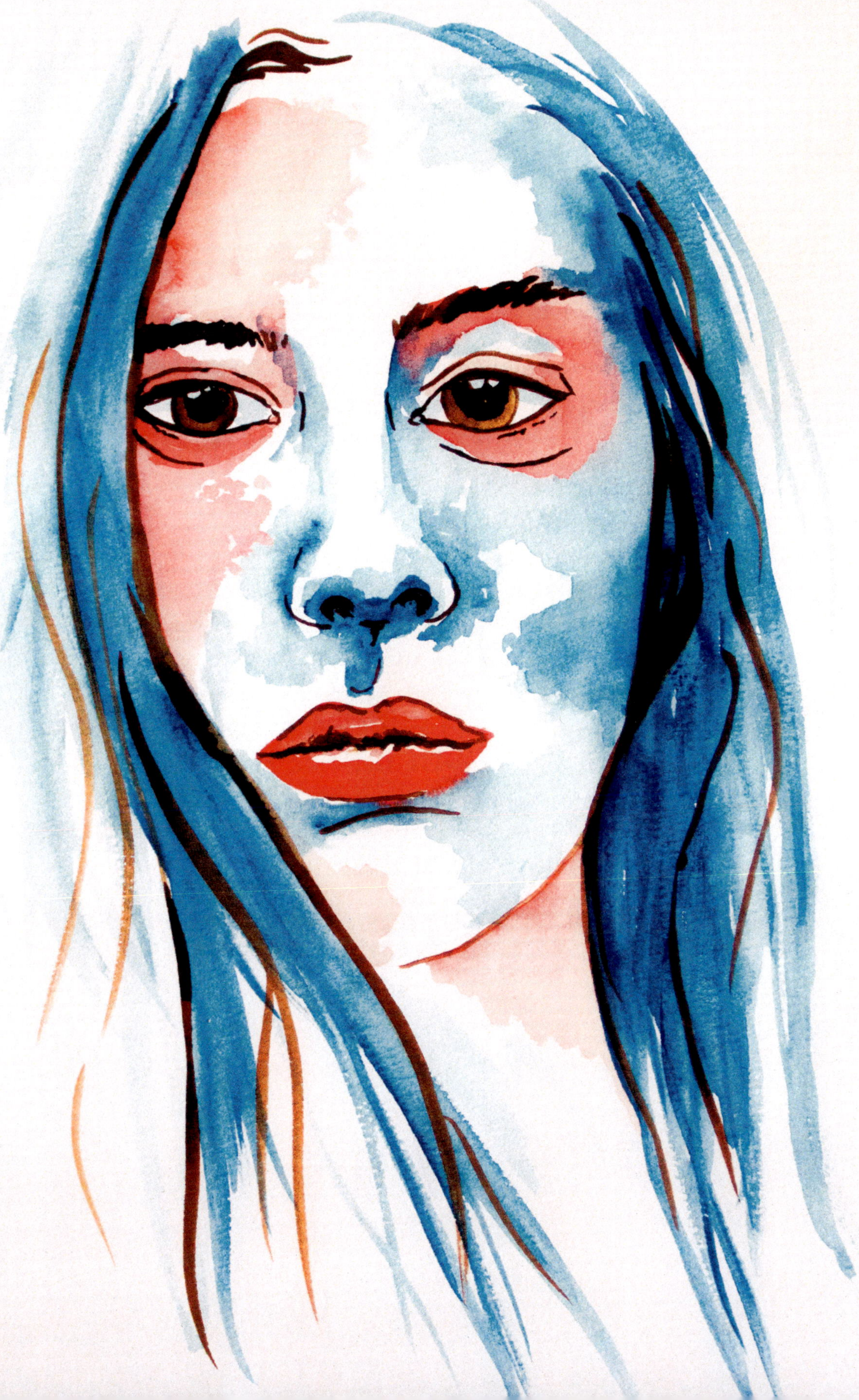

Tryphena and Tryphosa

Rome was the capital of the Roman Empire. It was a city where people from very different places, races, and ideologies converged. But all of them were under the strict laws of the empire. For the Roman Empire, not everyone was equal. There were people who had higher positions and others whose value in society was much lower. Those who were higher could enjoy a more comfortable life. Those who were lower were destined to work their whole lives. In the culture of the Roman Empire, working in general was frowned upon. It was much better to be served and recognized by others.

But in the church of Rome, it was different. Tryphena felt fortunate to be part of such a different group of people, where they could be together in the same space and worship God without paying attention to the differences. In the church, working for the Lord was a privilege, not something that made you inferior. Tryphena was happy to be a part of it, even as a woman. It was the same for Tryphosa, who was also part of the congregation. Tryphena and Tryphosa were sisters; they had grown up together, and they had remained very close all their lives. They had both heard about Jesus and decided they wanted to follow Him. Now, the two of them were part of the church of Rome and had the privilege of working for the Lord, helping the rest of the brothers and sisters, and participating in whatever was planned there. For Tryphena and Tryphosa, serving the Lord was indeed a privilege, but even more so doing it alongside a person as special as a sister. God had prepared a special place where the two could work together.

In a society where working and serving others was a sign of inferiority, God used two women whom He recognized for their good work for Him and whom we still remember today for their example and courage.

Romans 16:12

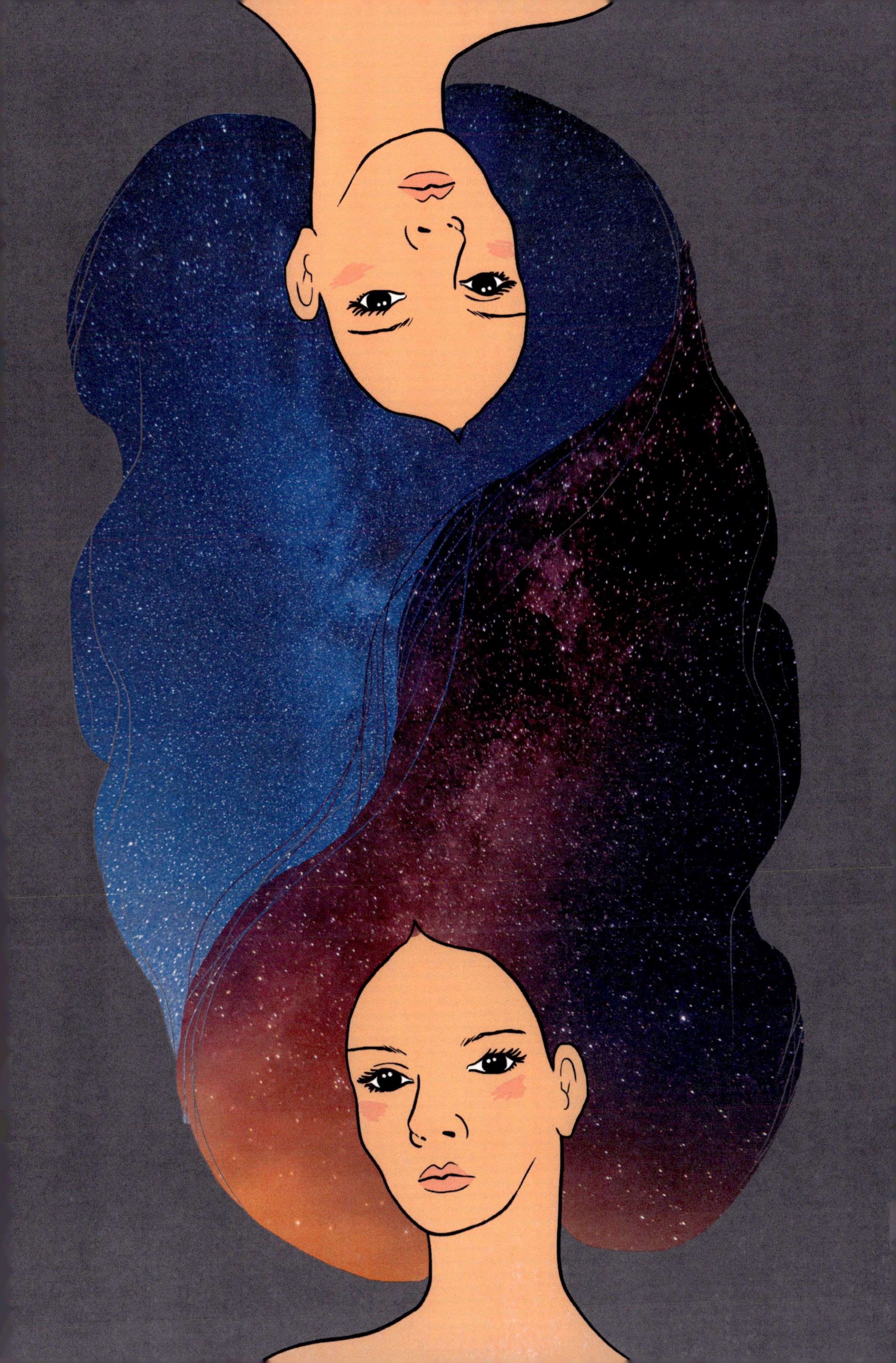

Persis

Someone was holding the papyrus in his hands as he read aloud. Everyone listened attentively while imagining Paul himself reciting those words. Some Christians in the church of Rome, like Persis, already knew him; they were excited to have received a letter from him. In his letter, Paul spoke about how God, through Jesus, brought salvation to all humanity. He talked about how the Jews had tried, for years, to follow the laws and commandments to fit in as part of God's people, but even then, it was impossible to redeem their broken relationship with God. But now, all humanity, both Jews and Gentiles, could become part of God's people through Jesus, who erased any barrier in their relationship with God.

Persis was thinking about this when she suddenly heard her name. She raised her eyebrows slightly; the letter said, "greet my dearest sister Persis, who has worked very hard in the Lord." Persis wasn't used to anyone mentioning her by name in front of a crowd or having her work recognized. This was something that regularly happened to men, but to her, a woman? Persis smiled humbly. She remembered that while Jesus lived on earth, He taught a group of disciples who followed Him everywhere. She knew He had also allowed a group of women to go with Him. Persis had always found this strange; teachers normally only accepted men as students. Persis had been amazed that women were also accepted and recognized by Jesus. And now, here she was, more than 20 years later, mentioned and recognized for her work for God in one of the letters that thousands of Christians would continue to read long afterward. Persis had never felt important in her society; she had never thought she could have any kind of impact on others; she had always felt inferior for the simple fact of being a woman. Now, however, she knew that this was her place, a place where she felt accepted and valued, a place she was a part of and knew she would belong to forever.

Romans 16:12

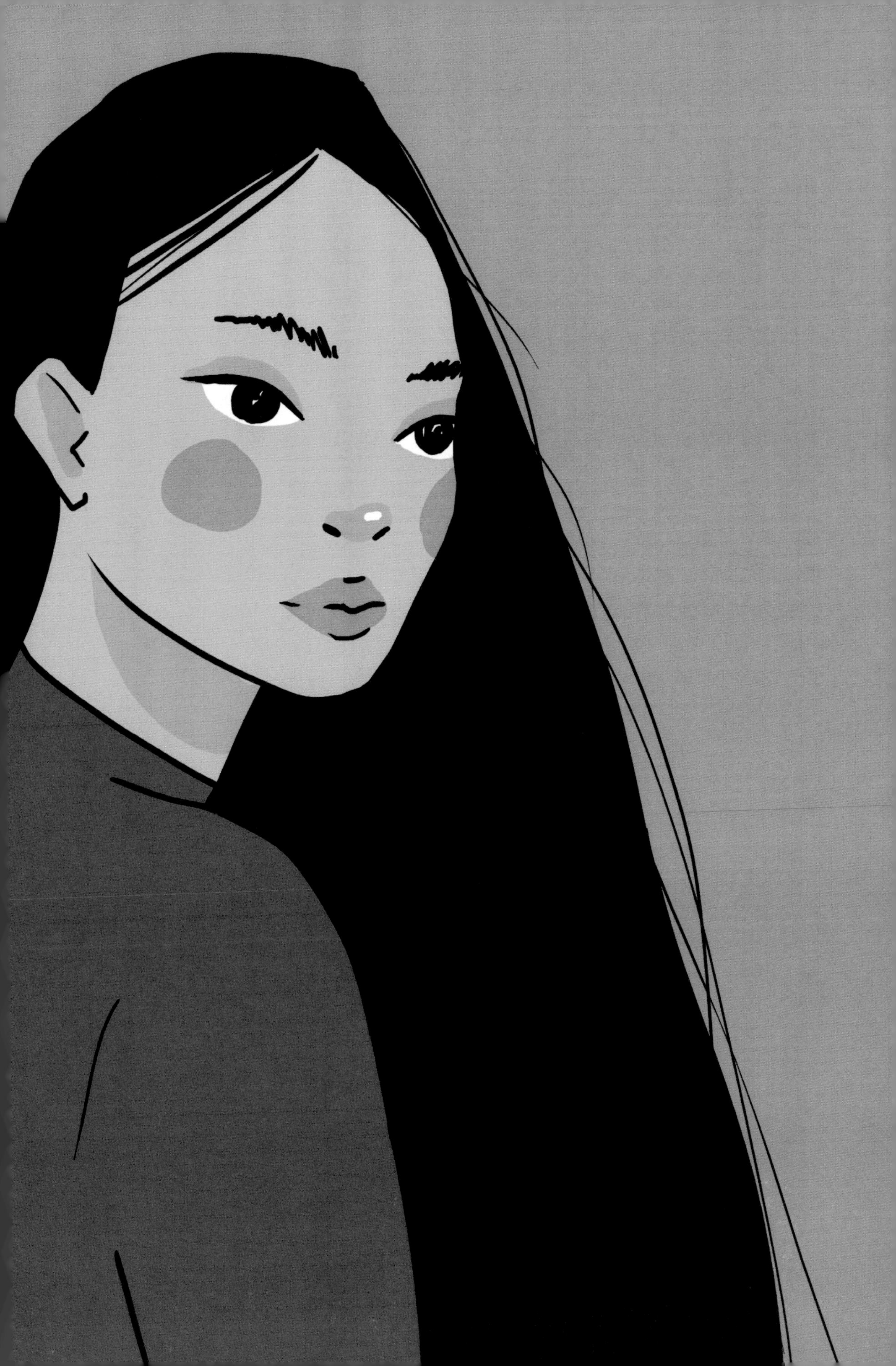

Mary of Rome

Everything seemed to be ready. Mary looked around, checking that nothing needed attending to and making sure that the brothers and sisters who were taking care of the last preparations didn't need help, while some stragglers were still entering the door. She had woken up happy that morning, excited and joyful to share and worship God with other Christians. It was a privilege for her to help the church continue, although she couldn't do it as much due to her age.

Rome was a noisy and constantly busy city. The church of Rome sometimes was too. As in all churches, there were sometimes conflicts and difficulties to go through. Mary noticed two brothers who were talking; she smiled when she saw that they finally seemed to have overcome their differences. Some of the Christians in Rome were Jews, like her. They had been raised thinking they were God's special people and no one else could be a part of that. But most in Rome were not Jews, but Gentiles. At first, Mary had a hard time understanding it too; however, she accepted that Jesus, with His death, opened a direct path to God for anyone who wanted to take it; everyone, not just the Jews. Of course, this was difficult to understand for many Jews, who still felt they were the special people chosen by God since Abraham and Sarah.

When everyone was seated at the table, Mary watched as a sister poured wine into her glass. The bread was also laid on the tablecloth. She knew what sharing bread and wine together represented: that Jesus had given His own life for us so that together, Jew and Gentile, we might enjoy eternal life with God. And there they were sitting at the table, Gentiles, Jews, young, old, women, men, all a part of that special group of the family of God. Mary's eyes sparkled as she raised her glass.

Romans 16:6

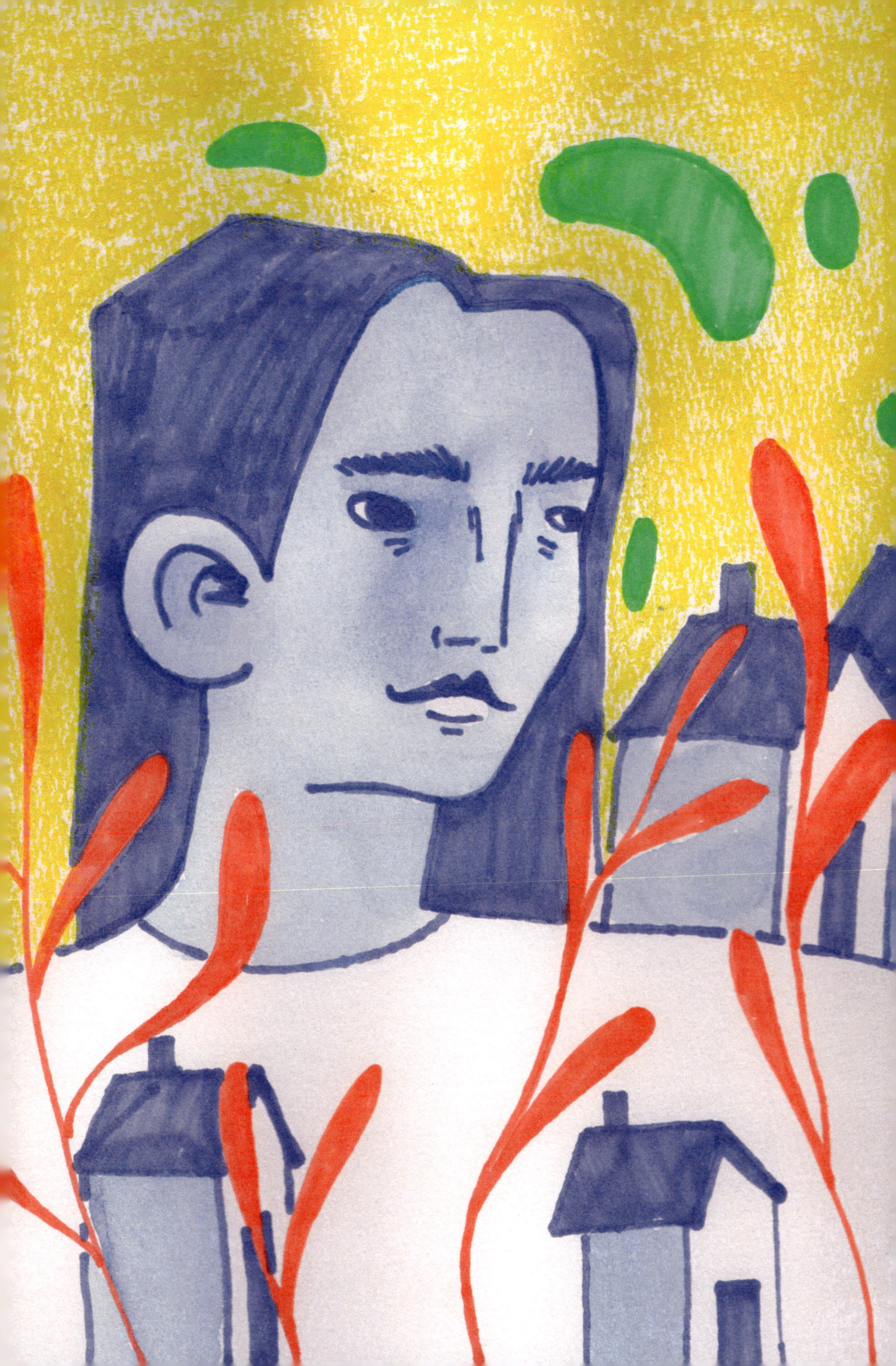

Julia

The last few months had been very confusing for Julia. Some years before, the Roman emperor had forced all the Jews to leave Rome, but fortunately, they were able to return after a few years. So now, there were Jews in the same church that Julia belonged to. Julia wasn't Jewish, but she knew that the Jews had been fortunate enough to be God's special people for many years; she loved hearing about how God had protected them and done wonderful things in their history.

Julia's life had been impacted by a special Jew: Jesus of Nazareth, who had lived for several years and given His life to receive the punishment we all deserved. Julia had never felt so loved as when she learned that someone had been willing to do something like this so that she, too, could be part of that special people of God. She was grateful that she could be a part of the church even though she wasn't one of them.

However, since the Jews had returned to Rome, the church's situation had become very tense. Some Jews believed that the Gentiles had to take on Jewish traditions. Non-Jewish Christians, for their part, were opposed because they claimed they were free to make that decision themselves. Julia didn't quite know what to think. She was afraid of making a mistake, but she didn't know the best option.

Paul's letter came at a time of great need. Paul encouraged the church to be a united group without divisions. He encouraged them to focus on what was really important and said that the more mature should help those with less experience. Those words brought peace to the congregation; whenever any kind of dispute began, they only needed to unroll the papyrus written by Paul and reread it again. Julia was thankful that she had those written words, inspired by God, to turn to in times of need.

Romans 16:15

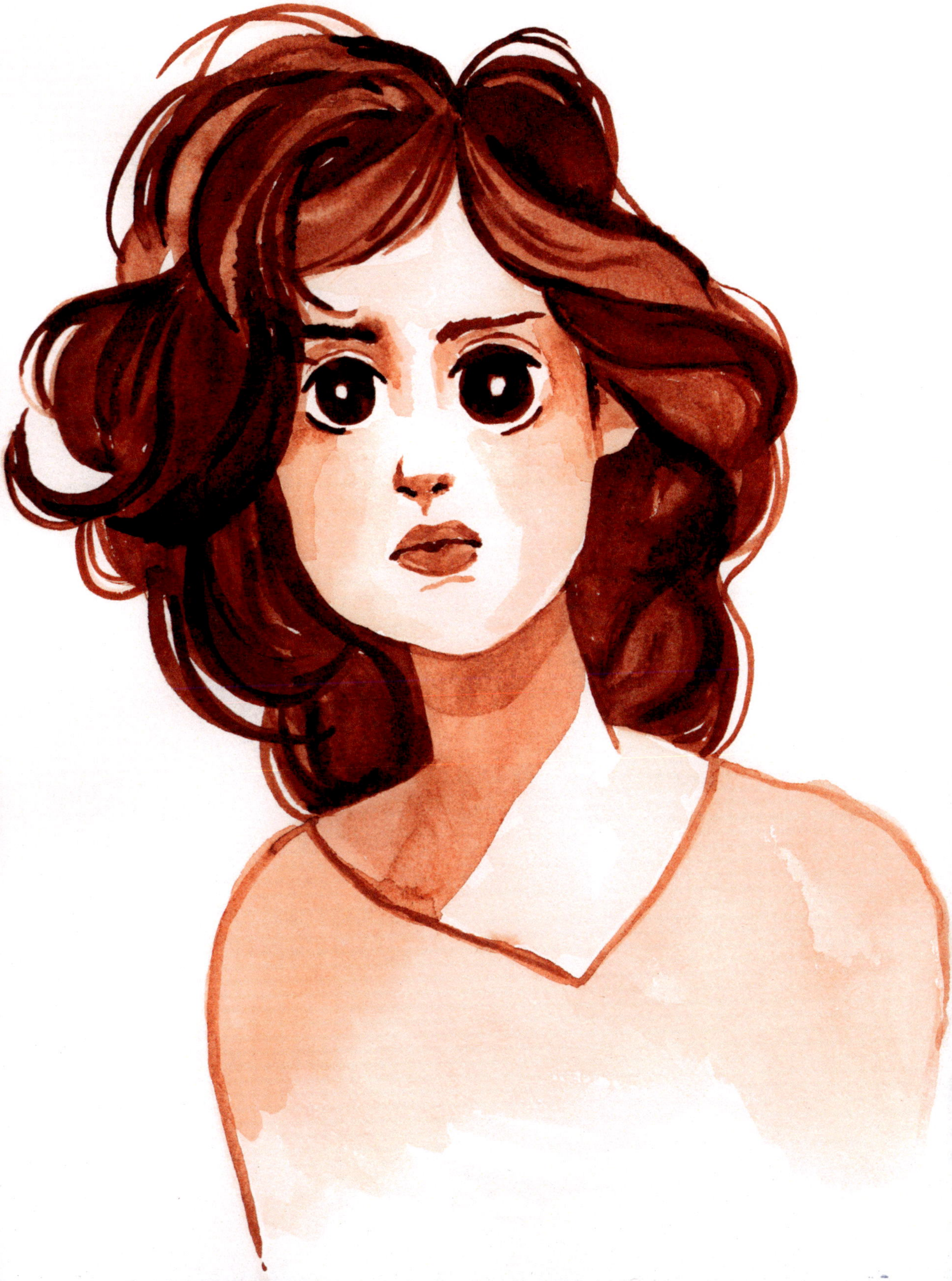

Apphia

Apphia saw her husband Philemon jump up. Immediately, she realized that someone had just arrived at their house. She could hardly believe it when she realized it was Onesimus. How dare he return? After everything that scoundrel had done to them.

Apphia and Philemon were a wealthy couple from Colossae. They were good friends of Paul and Epaphras. They were also an exemplary Christian family, and the church in Colossae met in their home. Like many Roman families at that time, they had slaves in their service. Onesimus was one of them. But long ago, Onesimus had long ago escaped from the house after doing something terrible. Philemon was very upset. According to Roman law, in this case, it was his right to send Onesimus to jail or even kill him if he wanted.

Onesimus humbly approached Philemon and Apphia and handed them a letter from Rome. It was a letter from Paul. They quickly opened it and began to read it. In the letter, Paul told them that Onesimus was now a Christian. Apphia looked at Onesimus, barely able to believe it. But that wasn't all; Paul asked them to release Onesimus and forgive him. Paul himself was willing to pay the punishment that Onesimus deserved. In addition, Paul, with his words, showed them how Onesimus was now just another Christian, just like them, and asked them from that moment on to treat him not as a slave, but as a brother, as part of their own family. For a moment, Apphia and Philemon were so stunned they couldn't say a single word.

Apphia knew how difficult this was for her husband. She herself would've never imagined that she could call one of her slaves her brother. No one in all of Rome would have thought to spare a slave like him, much less free him and treat him like… a brother? That seemed totally out of the question. Apphia met her husband's eyes. She knew what he was thinking despite the lack of expression on his face. Jesus Himself had offered His own life to set everyone free: Jew and Gentile, male and female, free and slave. Yes, it defied all logic. How great was the love of God! Much bigger than they could have ever imagined.

Philemon 1

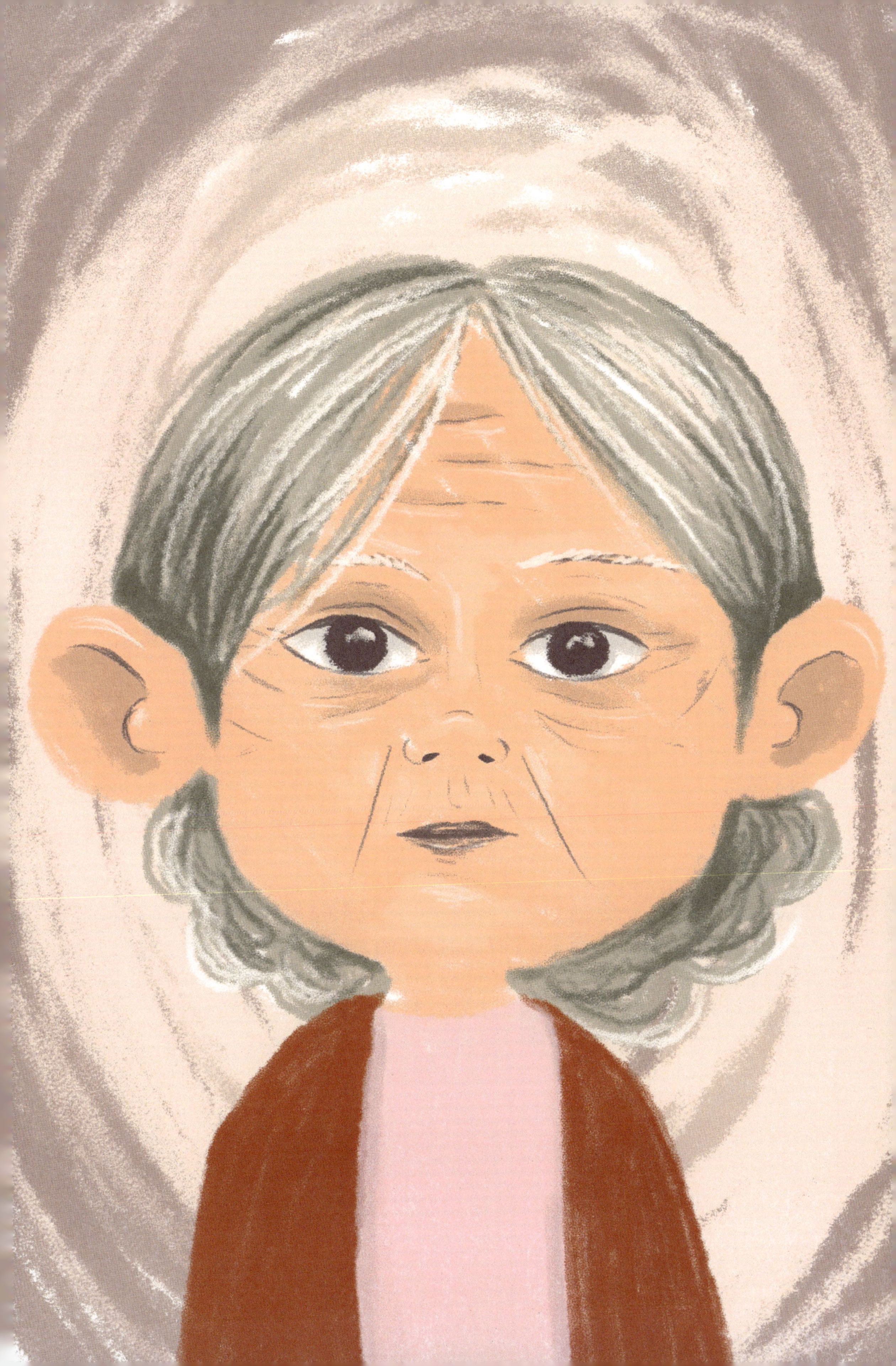

Euodia

The church in Philippi had grown tremendously since the gospel reached this area of the Mediterranean. Little by little, the words Paul shared with a group of women spread among the city's inhabitants. The women shared the message with each other, and thus it also reached their husbands. More and more people gathered to pray and worship God, so the number of Christians in Philippi grew.

Euodia was one of those women. For years she had worked so that more people could know what Jesus had done for them. God hadn't cared about her past or where she came from. Despite not being part of His special people, she could still be one of His daughters. She had met many others just like her. People with whom she talked about the new hope in their lives, met to pray, studied the Word of God, and sang praises. Some had become more than friends: brothers and sisters with whom to share life. Syntyche was one of those close people. Together they had spent many hours sharing with others what they had found in God. They had laughed and cried together. They had shared the joy of being God's daughters.

But now things were not the same. A terrible argument had ended years of friendship and work together for the Lord. Although they saw each other frequently, they preferred not to look each other in the eye and tried to avoid each other at all costs. Everyone knew that it was a difficult matter to solve. Everyone, including Paul. Recently, Paul had dedicated a few words to them, encouraging them to reconcile. Euodia had been thinking about it a lot. She still didn't understand why Syntyche was so stubborn. But what if she was too? Was it worth keeping her distance? Couldn't they work together again like before? Perhaps they didn't even need to agree on everything, just know, as they already knew, that God loved them both and had rescued them to make them His children. They were part of the same family; despite everything, they were sisters. Yes, they definitely had to fix this situation.

Philippians 4:2-3

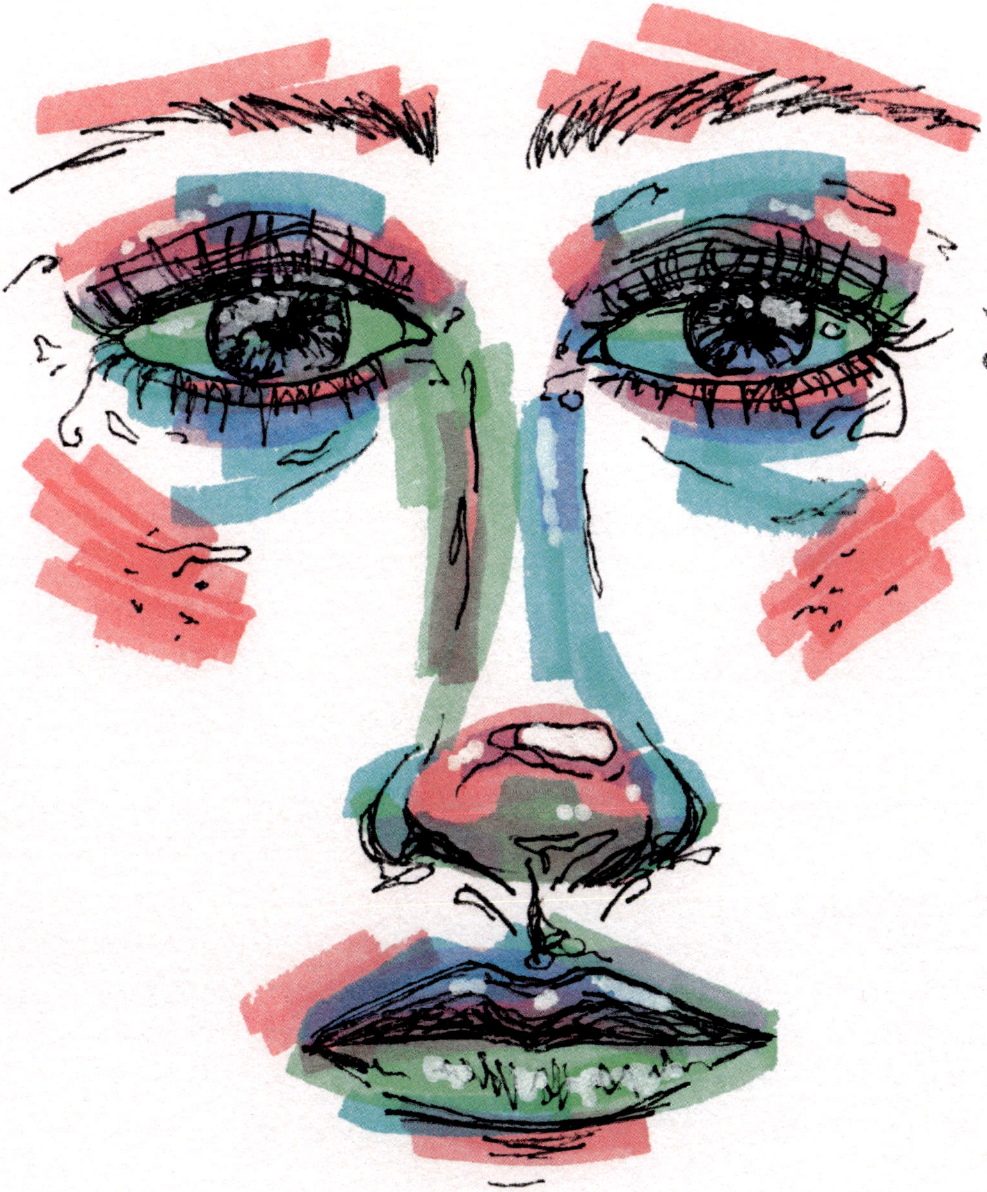

Syntyche

Syzygus came quietly and sat down beside Syntyche. He waited in silence for a few moments, then began to speak. He talked about the old days. He talked about the years when nothing could stop them. The message of Jesus was alive; it ran like a current inside them. It urged them not to stop. To share the news of the death and resurrection of Jesus with all those whenever they had the opportunity. Jesus was alive. And thanks to that, anyone who wanted could be, too. Anyone could stop living a sad and meaningless life to become a follower of Christ. Christ's followers had life. This special thing gave them hope for the future. Something stronger than anguish, suffering, or even death. It was passion. A shared passion.

Syntyche remembered those times, and something began to sizzle happily inside her. Yes, she remembered the passion. The same she had shared with others. With Paul himself, also with Clement, with Euodia... When the image of Euodia appeared in her mind, something inside her turned off again. No, not with Euodia. She no longer shared anything with Euodia.

Syzygus continued speaking. This passion. It was important. It was more important than many other things. They couldn't let it be extinguished. Because when it faded, when the desire to serve God and share Him with others was no longer there, it was because something else had taken its place. And that wasn't good. Syzygus spoke with affection, like someone who wants to help, like someone who cares about others. He really wanted Syntyche's old passion to spring forth again with the same intensity. And that it also would grow again in Euodia. They were good women, they loved God, and they loved others, but they had let something else take a place it shouldn't. They had lost that common enthusiasm that should unite all Christians. Syntyche considered Syzygus' words. If she was honest with herself, she had to admit he was right. She had let her passion fade. She had to bring it back. It wasn't just her passion. It was a common passion.

Philippians 4:2-3

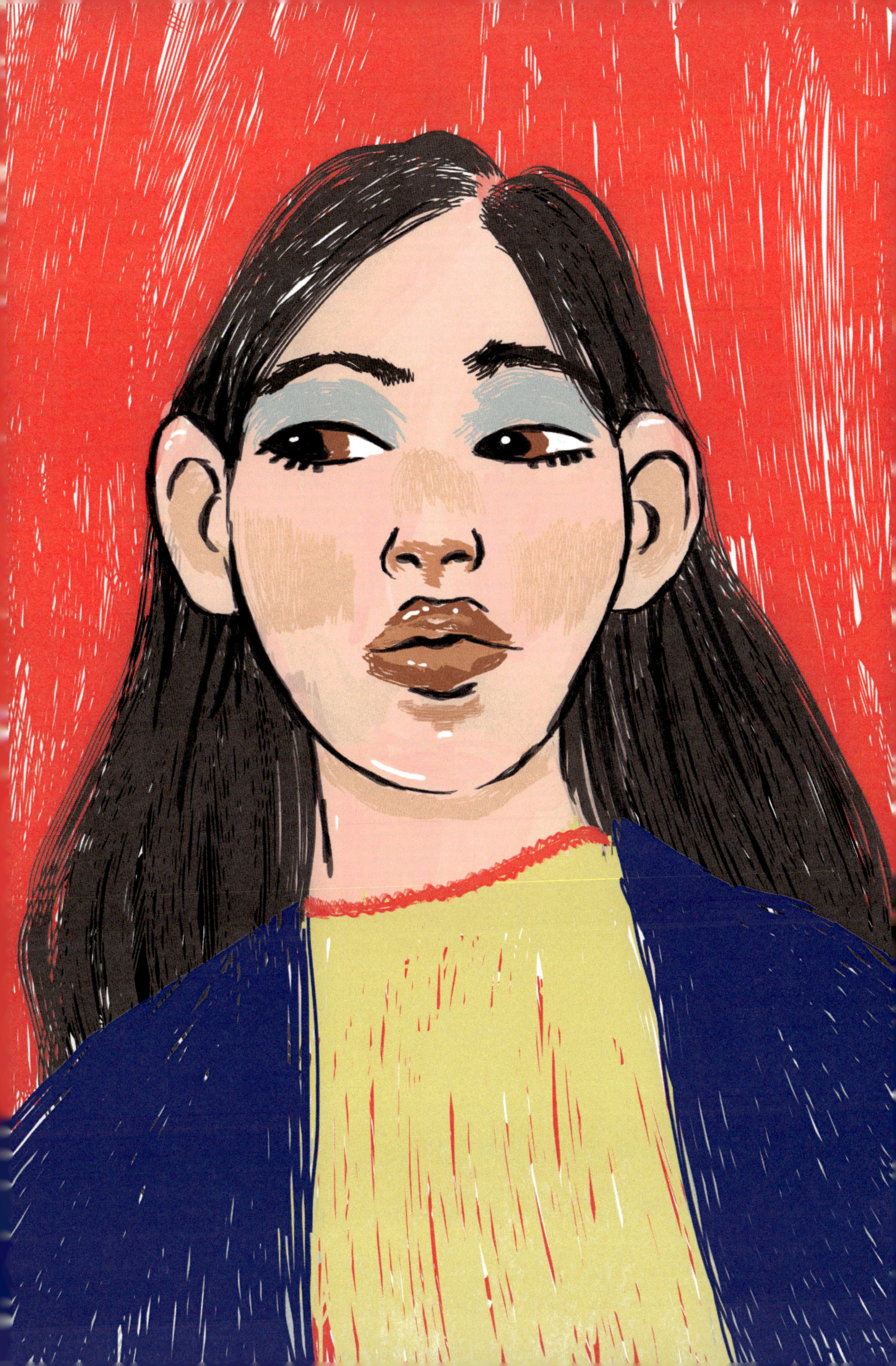

Lois

Some children are lucky enough to have at least one of their grandmothers nearby. Some grandmothers also become role models for their grandchildren, so their mark remains ingrained in their lives even after they are gone. Lois was one of these grandmothers.

Lois was a woman of faith. She lived according to what she believed. She believed in God and considered His principles one of the most important things in her daily life. It was not a faith that appeared on only a few days or in certain moments. Lois lived her love for God and her service to others every day, at all times and in all places, both inside and outside her home. Timothy, her grandson, watched her daily; even without realizing it, he learned from her. From his grandmother, Timothy learned to trust in God, to give Him a primary place in his life, to love others, and to live each day as God pleases. These qualities can't be easily faked, especially behind closed doors when no one else seems to see us. Both his grandmother Lois and his mother Eunice were good examples to Timothy as he became a strong and committed Christian. That was how, little by little, from watching these two women do the same things day after day, Timothy learned too.

Many years later, when Timothy no longer lived with his grandmother, he maintained the sincere faith that had characterized his grandmother Lois in his own life. Timothy also lived out his love and service to God and others every day, at all times and in all places, both inside and outside his home. Many times, in any situation in life, he remembered the words of his grandmother speaking to him about God or advising him to always stay on His path. If someone who knew Lois were to meet Timothy years later, they would be able to see in him the same characteristics once seen in his grandmother.

2 Timothy 1:5

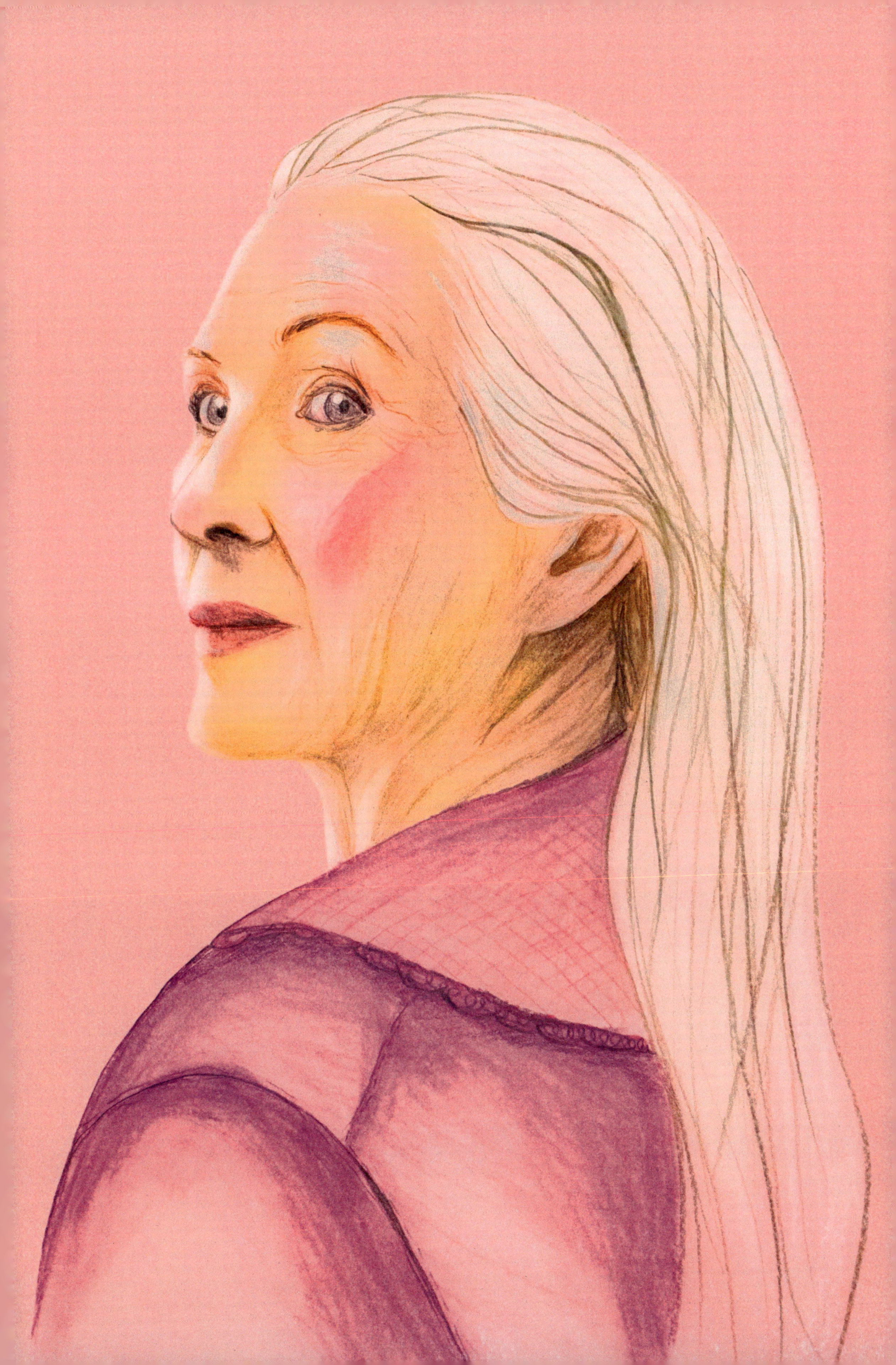

Eunice

Eunice was a young Jewish girl who dreamed of getting married and being a mother, like many other young women from Lystra, where she lived. One day she met a Greek boy with whom she saw her dream come true. But often, dreams come true differently than we expect. Not everything in Eunice's life was as she had imagined; there were many things she would've liked to change. But Eunice kept going and held on tightly to her faith. She trusted God to help her, and He did.

Eunice woke up each morning determined to live a life that honored God. She studied the scriptures and put her faith into practice day by day. Many people around her were watching her, especially her young son, Timothy. He grew up seeing in his mother an example of a woman with a strong faith founded on the Word of God. And he himself applied that to his own life, becoming an obedient, humble son and a true servant of God.

Every week at her church, different people would come up to Eunice and say, "Oh, how mature your son Timothy is!" or "Look how he's growing; what a good boy he is." Eunice smiled at the great man her son was becoming.

Years later, Paul, one of her son Timothy's best friends, realized how important Eunice had been in Timothy becoming the great gospel servant he had become when he was still very young. Despite being a time when women had few opportunities to influence society, Eunice was influential in the spread of Christianity and the church's growth in Ephesus thanks to the great influence her life and faith had on the son she had raised with so much love.

Acts 16:1,
2 Timothy 1:5

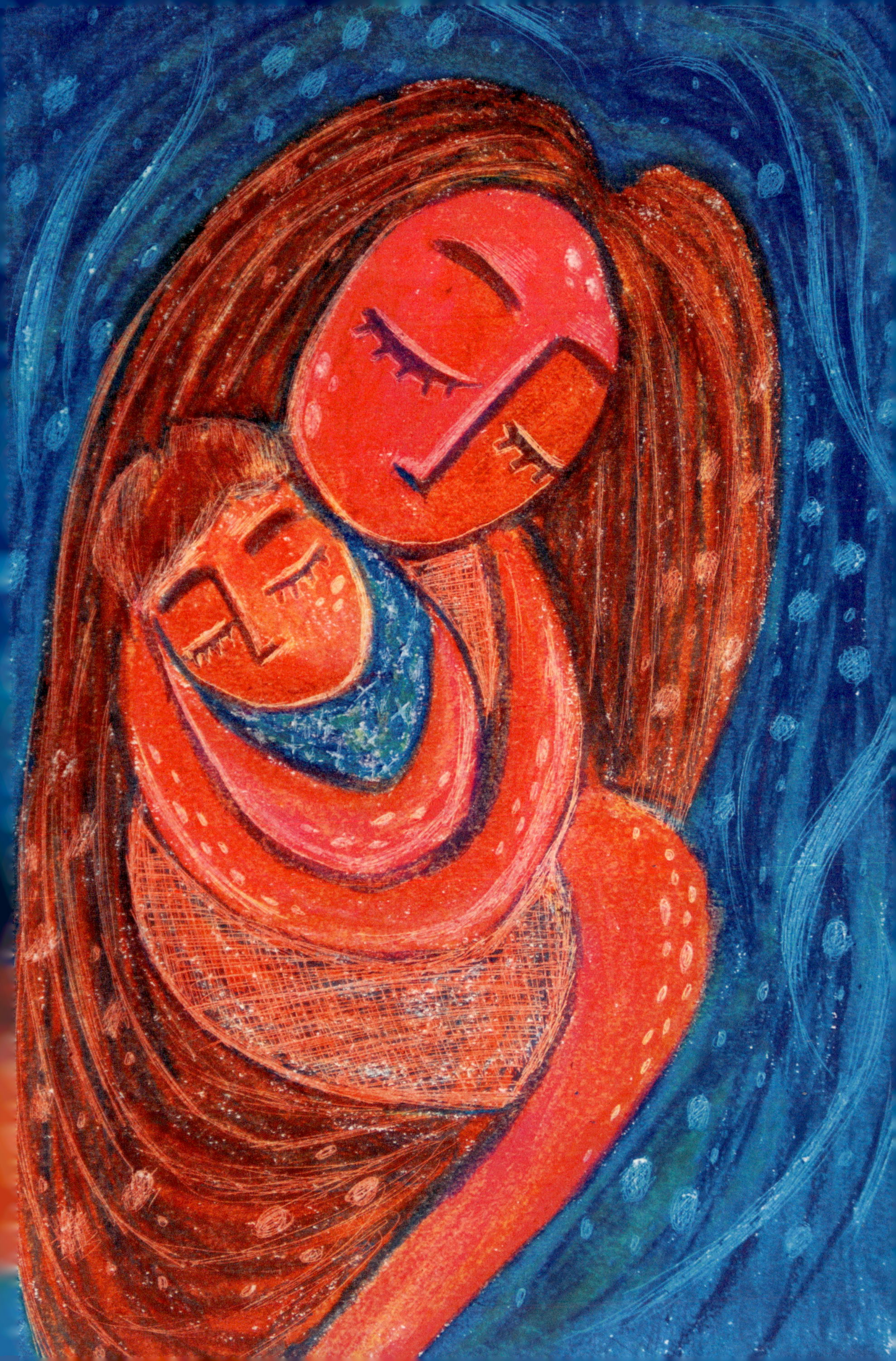

Claudia

Claudia hastened her steps until she completely left behind the place. She passed the last control where the Roman soldiers guarded the entrance to the prison in Rome, and finally on the street, breathed calmly. Every time she visited Paul in prison, she had this same unpleasant feeling. Today she was especially sad to have seen Paul in such unfortunate conditions. Paul was awaiting trial, but from what he had shared, he didn't have much hope of being released. On top of that, Paul didn't seem to be in very good health lately. Claudia was afraid of how winter might affect him. The prison was a very cold place, and the conditions there were terrible for his health.

Many Christians had forgotten about Paul. They were actually ashamed of him and didn't want to be associated with a criminal. Even though Paul, far from being a criminal, had been arrested precisely for sharing the gospel. Claudia was sorry that others thought that way. Sometimes she was also afraid of what might happen to her if she kept visiting Paul. She knew she was taking a risk. Besides, she didn't even want to imagine how her contacts from the Roman aristocracy would react if they saw her enter that place to see Paul. But she knew how important it was to keep visiting, encouraging, and reminding him that he was not alone. Even though Paul knew perfectly well that Jesus was with him. Paul had done so much for others. His entire life had been given completely to others. He had fought and worked for so many people, and he had made an effort for them to know Jesus. Now was the time for others to support and be there for him.

Claudia walked firmly; she would continue visiting him whenever she could. She would continue encouraging and caring for other Christians regardless of their situation. Claudia could see in Paul that when a Christian suffers, God directly strengthens him in a special way. Suffering with Paul was not something she wanted to avoid; it was something that brought her even closer to Jesus and His love.

2 Timothy 4:21

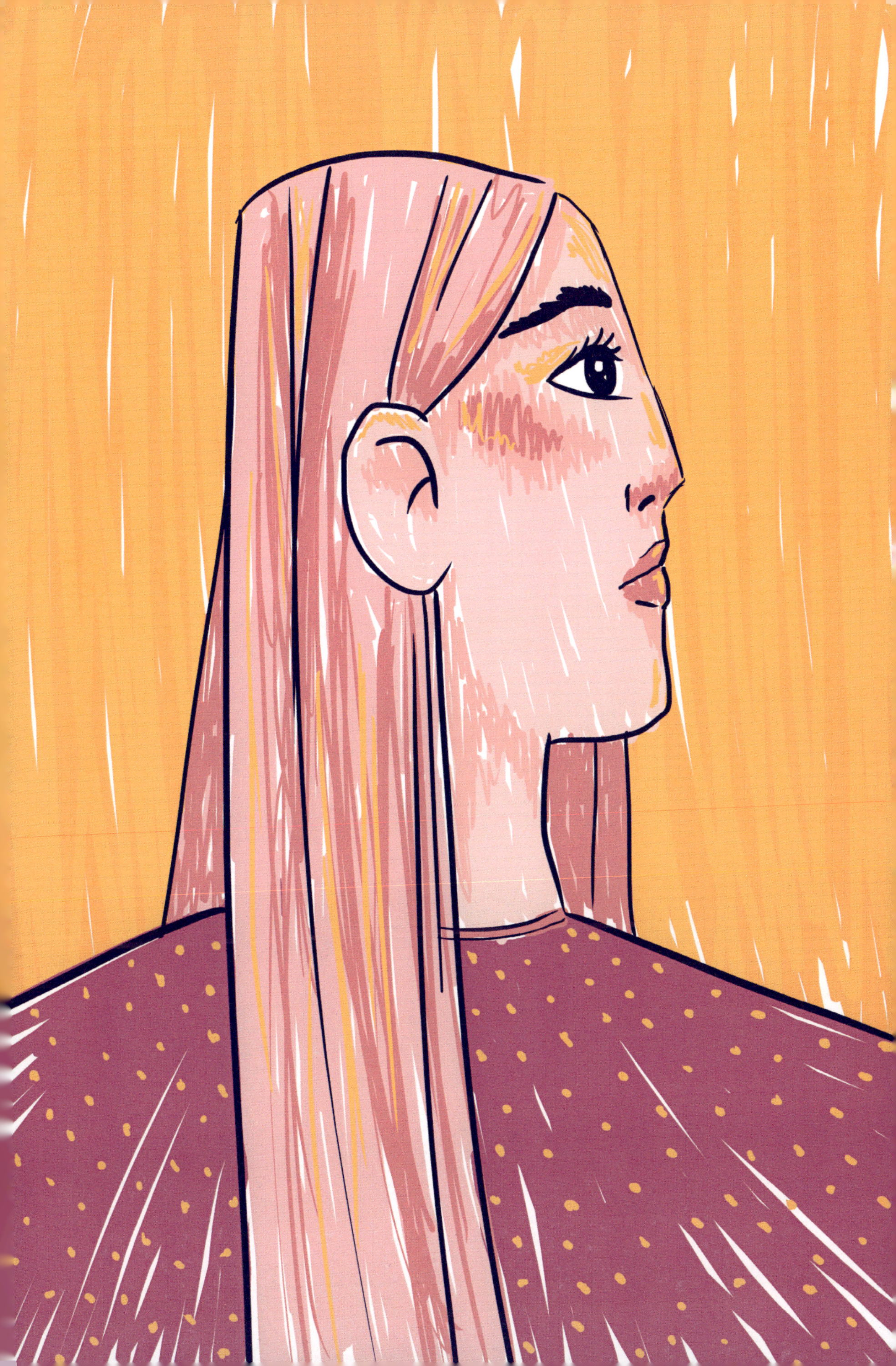

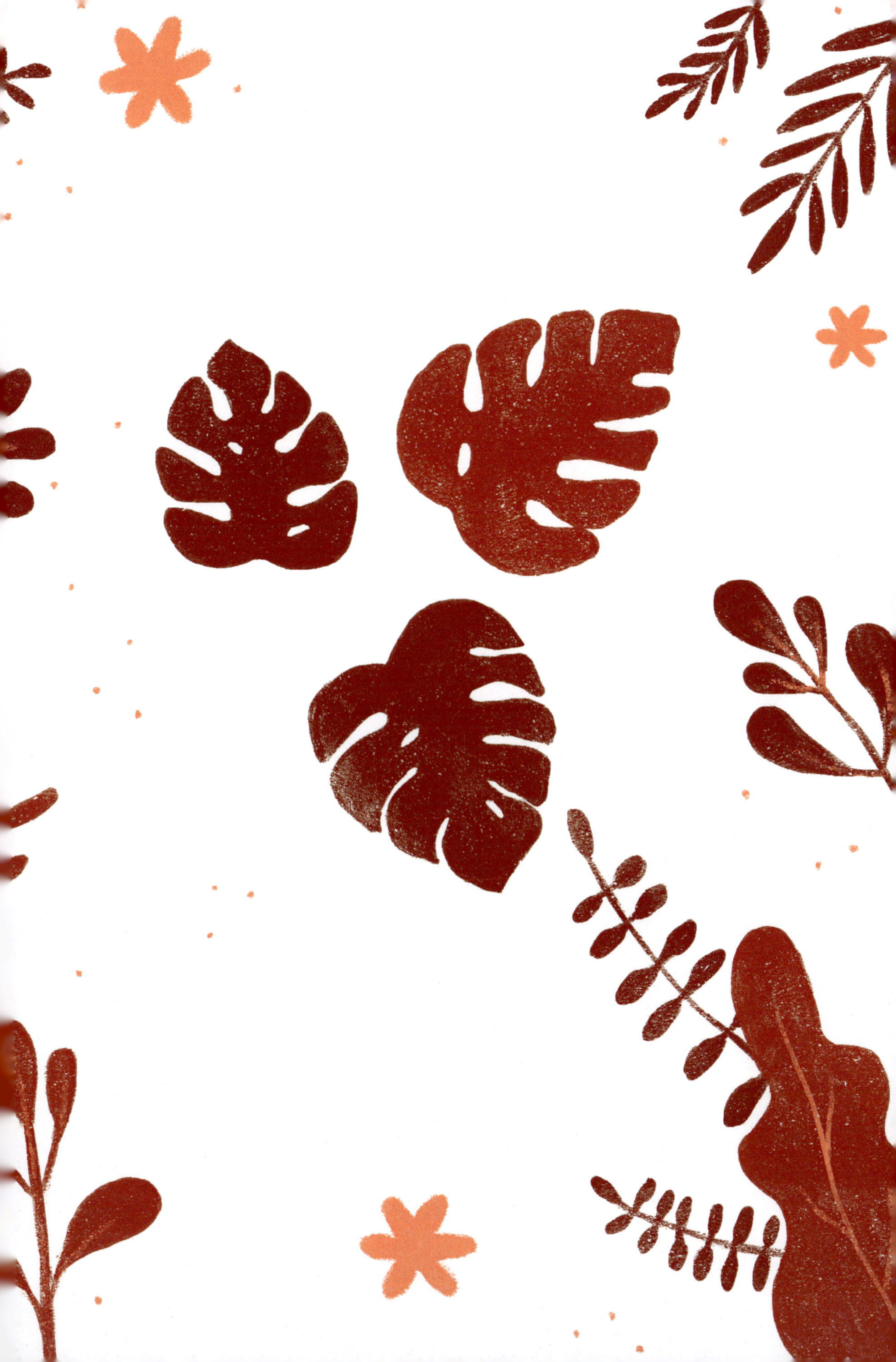

Made in the USA
Columbia, SC
01 June 2023

477ef2c0-59a0-484f-8f8f-07c1ecbbf2b5R02